PRAIS[barcode M000098055]

LEADERSHIP MAGIC

"*Leadership Magic* is a profoundly integrated collage of outstanding leadership essentials. I am more deeply connected with the leader in me when utilizing the tools in this book."
    Rev. David K. Hollowell, Pastor

"Valore-Caplan has created a refreshing management coda that blends relationships and action to create spiritual as well as tangible rewards. *Leadership Magic* is thought-provoking reading for anyone interested in nurturing a high performance organization."
    Pete Neidecker, President, MedSource/InstruMed

"*Leadership Magic* is for those who long to see change that begins with respect, authenticity, cooperation, trust, and the essential exchange between growth of the individual and growth of the group."
    Carl Hollander, M.A., Ed.D., T.E.P.
    Director, Hollander Institute for Human Development and Family Growth

"Change agents need effective tools to transform the "herding cats" experience to one of shared passion, focus, and direction. I use *Leadership Magic* with my group of wildly diverse and talented individuals to do just that."
    Robert Collett, President, Techniku, Inc.

"During the chaos and confusion of starting a new business venture, I found inspiration in the honesty and directness of *Leadership Magic*. Ben Valore-Caplan reminded me that leadership is not a single event or series of events, but a way of life that we can all choose to follow."
    Cheryl Black, Vice President of Marketing, espoke.com

"The magic concept of leveraging diversity has challenged me to value and utilize the skills, talents, and perspectives of our organization's unique members. *Leadership Magic* captivates the imagination while leading your heart and spirit to continuous leadership enhancement."

Ron Konrath, Manager, IBM Groupware/GWA Services

"When a leader tackles the task of structuring or restructuring the organization for maximum performance, nothing has as much potential to facilitate the process as the concept in *Leadership Magic* of aligning the personal and organizational missions."

George W. Dorry, Ph.D., Psychologist
Director, The Attention and Behavior Center

"As a Federal manager who has participated in numerous trainings and read many books on management, I found Valore-Caplan's material exceptional and timely. *Leadership Magic* captures the essence of what others have alluded to. It will inspire everyone who reads it, regardless of where they stand in their organization or life as leaders."

Rafael Zambrano, Manager, U.S.D.A., F.N.S., Denver, CO

WORDWORKS PRESS

LEADERSHIP MAGIC

LEADERSHIP MAGIC

PRACTICAL TOOLS
FOR CREATING EXTRAORDINARY
ORGANIZATIONS

BEN VALORE-CAPLAN

WORDWORKS PRESS • DENVER

Leadership Magic. Copyright © 1999 by Ben Valore-Caplan. All rights reserved. Printed in the United States of America. No part of this book may be used or reproduced in any manner whatsoever without written permission except in the case of brief quotations embodied in critical articles or reviews. For information, address Wordworks Press, 1980 South Pearl Street, Denver, CO 80210.

Design by Amie and Ben Valore-Caplan

Library of Congress Cataloging-in-Publication Data

Valore-Caplan, Ben
    Leadership magic: practical tools for creating extraordinary
organizations/ Ben Valore-Caplan.—1st ed.
    Includes bibliographical references and index.
    ISBN 0-9671957-0-5
    Library of Congress Catalog Card Number: 99-90975

First Edition: September, 1999

DEDICATION

To my teachers,
for their gifts of
time, energy, wisdom,
and heart.

ACKNOWLEDGMENTS

This book represents the collaborative contributions of many talented people. Some have been role models and mentors who have taught me powerful leadership skills. Others have read previous versions of the manuscript and offered valuable feedback. Their insights have enriched what you are about to read, making it more accessible, helpful, and eloquent. I appreciate the contributions of these many individuals, and though I could hardly list everyone who has taught me, I thank some of those who have made me a better person, and thus made *Leadership Magic* a better book.

I offer a warm thank you to Cheryl Black, Benita Campbell, Marty Caplan, Rob Collett, Lewis Daniels, George Dorry, Louis Fine, Hank Fisher, Chris Gibbons, Bill Harris, David Hix, Brian Hoal, Carl Hollander, David Hollowell, Don Jones, Tom Kaesemeyer, Don Kipp, Ron Konrath, Lois Loofburrow, Ad Lopez, Richard Lyons, Jen Mayer-Sandoval, Dennis Mead-Shikaly, Margaret Metzger, Gordon Miller, Curtis Mitchell, Pete Neidecker, Dennis Ondrejka, Jean Patrick, Jim Peterson, Gordon Pierce, Tom Pitner, Dan Ritchie, Susan Schell, Sheila Silverman, Susanne States, David Sullivan, Rob Susmark, Rich Tosi, Jim White, Rafael Zambrano, and Mary Zellner.

I also honor a special group that has dared me to practice these leadership skills on a daily basis. The Summerbridge community has taught me by example that when people support, challenge, and inspire each other, we have the power to accomplish most any goal. I know so many heroes who possess every justification to settle for less than they deserve, yet remain committed to hard work, dedication, respect, fun, and, most of all, to excellence in learning. Each of you has earned my Spirit Stick.

To the courageous and committed men of The ManKind Project, I judge that I would not be here now without you. I hope that this book proves a worthy acknowledgment of the gifts you have so generously shared with me.

My family provided the first lessons about leadership, and has remained an essential part of my life. Around those very large tables, I have truly learned about diversity and conflict, communication and relationship, mission and risk-taking. Each of you intrigues and inspires me in your own way. This book is for our children and theirs.

And my loving wife, Amie. Talented artist, skilled leader, committed and loving friend. You dazzle me with your rare blend of creativity and intelligence. Without you, *Leadership Magic* would still be just an idea sketched in a notebook. I am fortunate to share life with one so skilled as a writer and artist. You have led me when I could not remember where I was going or why. May this bold risk be but one more that we take together.

Thank you all.

CONTENTS AT A GLANCE

TABLE OF CONTENTS

INTRODUCTION

RECOGNIZING LEADERSHIP MAGIC

THE SUPREME TRAGEDY OCCURS WHEN THEORY
OUTSTRIPS PERFORMANCE.

LEONARDO DAVINCI

Have you noticed that some organizations possess a special energy? They consistently do well. They pursue their goals so smoothly that their success seems magical. Maybe you have been part of such a group and felt the ease with which you were able to interact with others, the seamless way that responsibilities were shared, and the genuine cooperation that propelled the group forward. If only all group activities could be so successful! If only we knew how to create such magical synergy every time!

Fortunately, we *can* create this energy. All of the time? No, certainly not. But there are practices that leaders can use to challenge and invite people to perform ever closer to their fullest potential. Given effective tools and the courage to use them, leaders can create environments that elicit excellent performance from individuals and groups. They can help people tap their innate creativity, intelligence, and skill by enabling them to realize and express their fullest power. The closer people get to their personal and professional best, the closer their organizations come to fulfilling their missions. As the organization flourishes, its members become even more successful. Thus, leadership magic invites a win-win relationship between people and organizations. The rewards are sweet.

REWARDS OF LEADERSHIP MAGIC

➤ *Greater commitment to the organization and its mission*
➤ *Clearer expectations, roles, and responsibilities*
➤ *More constructive risk-taking*
➤ *Better retention of high-caliber people*
➤ *Higher quality decision-making and problem-solving*
➤ *More timely and effective response to potential crises*
➤ *Increased excitement and energy*
➤ *Better skilled people at every level of the organization*
➤ *More effective responses to internal and external change*
➤ *Greater initiative*
➤ *Increased productivity*

On the prevention side, leadership magic discourages apathy, sabotage, and passivity. It reduces distractions caused by unresolved conflict, misaligned missions, and repetitious mistakes. Leadership magic works on the underlying fabric of the organization. Rather than instituting a series of quick fixes, the practices described in this book enable a leader to impact the deeper culture of the organization. Thus, the benefits of leadership magic are sustainable over time and through various challenges.

Before I appear to promise the world, allow me a brief qualification. Sometimes a group of people "click" simply by chance. Perhaps they do so because of the personalities involved or the unique circumstances they face. Maybe some intangible force bonds people and makes their interaction so impressive. Sometimes groups just work out well. There will always be exceptional organizations whose magic is impossible to define. They are fun to watch and exciting to join.

However, most of us would rather not wait for fate to create the magic that can so dramatically impact our organizations. Fortunately, we can learn from those leaders who take deliberate steps to inspire organizational success. We can study their practices, adapt their tools, and create our own leadership magic.

As with any art, skill, craft, or science, leadership ability deepens with experience. You probably started long ago examining which practices inspire people to do their best and which ones undermine their performance. Ideally, you have developed a leadership style that fits your personality and your organization's needs. Like most of us, you probably have room to grow as well. Hopefully, this book can be a part of your growth.

WHY I HAVE WRITTEN *LEADERSHIP MAGIC*

NEVER DOUBT THAT A SMALL GROUP OF COMMITTED
INDIVIDUALS CAN CHANGE THE WORLD;
INDEED, THAT IS THE ONLY THING THAT EVER HAS.

MARGARET MEAD

In my vision of an ideal world, people challenge and support each other to become their personal best; they learn, grow, strive, achieve, and make the most of their opportunity together. In the process, the world becomes a more creative and loving place. My life's mission is to help create a world in which people have the freedom and opportunity to excel. Over the past ten years, I have helped start seven organizations or special projects and contributed significantly to the growth of many others. Along the way, I have encountered many excellent teachers in person and through books and other media. These role models and mentors have helped me develop an approach to leadership that balances the needs and gifts of people with the needs and gifts of organizations.

Leadership Magic is a manifestation of my mission. I have written it because I believe that every day we waste tremendous human potential, not necessarily on purpose, but because of how we practice or don't practice leadership in our lives and organizations. I am often heartened by people's creativity, just as I am angered by our capacity for destruction. With effective leadership, we can dramatically improve the likelihood that personal power will help to construct a richer, more dynamic world.

At my core, I am an idealist. I believe firmly that a healthy, responsible, and proactive community or organization can help elicit from people the best that they have to offer. I am also a realist; I recognize the limitations of trying to change others, as well as ourselves. Leaders cannot force people to grow or open their minds. They cannot eliminate cynicism or compel people to care about others. Leaders can simply invite growth and empathy; they can only make it safe and rewarding for people to work together effectively. Leaders who recognize the limitations of their power are more likely to be successful than are those who think they can control other people's learning process.

I have written *Leadership Magic* for leaders who have their feet grounded in the very real daily challenge of managing others, and their eyes sharply focussed on the highest potentials of people and organizations.

WHAT *LEADERSHIP MAGIC* OFFERS

KNOWING HOW THINGS WORK GIVES THE LEADER
MORE REAL POWER AND ABILITY THAN ALL THE
DEGREES OR TITLES THE WORLD CAN OFFER.

JOHN HEIDER

Leadership Magic focuses on four areas: Purpose, People, Process, and the ultimate goal, Performance. These areas build on each other to generate a powerful magic that can create a more successful organizational commitment and performance. The eight practices are intended for everyday use and can be integrated easily into the rhythm of an organization.

PRACTICES FOR CULTIVATING LEADERSHIP MAGIC

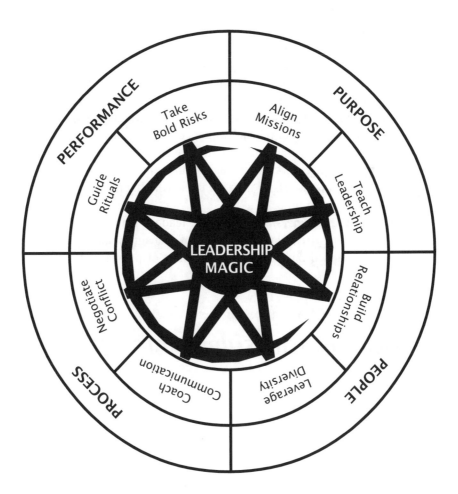

The eight core practices are guided by leadership challenges that capture the essence of how each practice impacts the organization. As the challenges reveal, leadership magic begins with intention and ends in action. Each step along the way intensifies the focus and power with which people act. Good intentions are not enough. Magic emerges only when purpose leads to right action.

LEADERSHIP CHALLENGES

ALIGN MISSIONS

Align the missions of people and the organization so that the success of one enhances the success of the other.

TEACH LEADERSHIP

Teach people how to become leaders of their own lives so that they can become leaders of others.

BUILD RELATIONSHIPS

Create an environment in which people invest in each other's success.

LEVERAGE DIVERSITY

Value and utilize the skills, talents, and perspectives of the organization's unique members.

COACH COMMUNICATION

Prepare people for success in their communication strategies.

NEGOTIATE CONFLICT

Leverage the power of conflict as a constructive tool for building a better organization.

GUIDE RITUALS

Energize and focus people through meaningful, inspiring activities.

TAKE BOLD RISKS

Lead people and organizations boldly into action.

Each chapter examines a different practice by introducing practical tools that leaders can use today in their organizations. As closure, each chapter offers self-reflection questions to help leaders assess their skills and opportunities for improvement. Heeding DaVinci's warning about the tragedy that results when theory outstrips performance, I have emphasized practical applications and kept the theoretical discussion to a minimum.

Those of you interested in researching why these practices are effective can find helpful resources listed in the appendix. Others will find that the best understanding comes from the experience of implementing these practices over and over again.

I've been using these tools for a long time, and they work. They elicit excellent performance from many people across various skill levels, ages, cultural backgrounds, and even degrees of motivation. At first, I hesitated to write this book because I don't yet possess reams of statistical data that would prove to some skeptics that these eight practices are *the ones* that create organizational magic. Actually, I doubt that they are the only ones. Certainly there are other leadership practices worth studying, yet I know by experience that these particular practices are effective. When these practices are present, I have been dazzled by what people can accomplish in relatively little time and with few resources. When they are absent, the most well-intentioned and well-endowed organizations can stumble, crumble, and fall. We all deserve to lead excellent organizations that take advantage of every opportunity and maximize one of their most important resources—their people. My intention here is to provide the practical tools and learning opportunities as directly and passionately as the printed page allows.

Many parts of the book may echo concepts articulated by other writers and leaders. Good teachers borrow material from the best teachers they can find, and as my acknowledgments indicate, I have been blessed to have so many excellent teachers. Hopefully, the unique framework I provide enhances their contributions and honors their intentions.

I am able to articulate many of the lessons in this book in part because, at one point or another, I have failed to practice them myself and learned their value the hard way. For example, I have found that aligning my personal mission with an organization's mission makes working with others much more pleasant. I emphasize the value of negotiating conflict because I felt the painful results of avoiding conflict before I developed the courage and skill to work with it. Rather than boring or distracting you with my learning process, I have tried to offer the essential lessons so that you can apply them as you best see fit. The process of learning is like mining for gold. We generally have to dig through layers of hard rock, break a lot of sweat, and literally move mountains before we find the precious treasures lying in wait. Out of respect for your time and energy, I intend this book to provide you with the gold rather than the tailings.

YOUR LEADERSHIP MAGIC IS NECESSARY

IF I AM NOT FOR MYSELF, WHO WILL BE FOR ME?
IF I AM ONLY FOR MYSELF, WHAT AM I?
IF NOT NOW, WHEN?

THE TALMUD

Imagine for a moment that the presence or absence of magic in your organization depends solely upon you. Because it very well might. Your organization sincerely needs you to put forth the best of your skills and energy, to help guide others toward personal excellence, and to risk leading your organization to even greater levels of performance. If you're not willing to do it, there might not be anyone else who will do so.

Neither your title nor your position can excuse you from exercising leadership magic. For the most part, these practices can be implemented from any vantage point in an organization. Both frontline staff members and senior vice-presidents can build relationships. Maintenance workers and CEOs are equally capable of negotiating conflict. Though leaders who possess less formal authority than their well-titled colleagues may have to be more creative in order to influence the organization, they can have just as dramatic an impact.

Too often, powerful people withhold the gifts they have to offer an organization. Some await an invitation to share their ideas. Others aren't sure their contributions would be valued. Still others are afraid to risk suggesting the wrong thing or making a mistake. If you are one of these people, now is an excellent time to take a different approach to leadership. There is no way to bring magic to an organization without taking personal and professional risks. As with any good risk, practicing leadership magic comes with commensurate reward. The people around you will perform more skillfully and enthusiastically, the organization will function more effectively, and you will grow as a person and leader.

I hope that you find these tools helpful and trust that you will share what you learn along the way. The world needs you to be your best, and you deserve it as well.

I PURPOSE

ALIGN MISSIONS
TEACH LEADERSHIP

IF WE DO NOT KNOW WHAT PORT WE'RE STEERING FOR,
NO WIND IS FAVORABLE.

SENECA

An organization without purpose drifts like a ship without a rudder. No matter how well the ship has been built and regardless of the quality of its crew, the wind and current take it wherever they like. The captain and crew can neither plan nor direct; they can only react to the whims of forces beyond their control. To create organizational magic, the captain not only ensures that the rudder works, but also makes sure that the crew intends to head in the same direction as the ship needs to go. Obvious? Perhaps. But the effective leader is not willing to carelessly gamble on the intentions of the crew or the fate of the organization.

A good captain teaches the crew how to sail the metaphorical ship. The captain recognizes that if he or she is the only one who can navigate through calm and storm, then the ship is always in danger, for what happens when the captain is unavailable, unprepared, or otherwise having a bad day? What if the bad day becomes a bad month? If no one else knows where—or why, how, or when—the ship is going, then how can it reach its destination when the captain is not around? Even an ever-present captain cannot be aware of every factor that contributes to a safe and speedy journey. Those who man the ropes and hold the wheel should be able to fulfill their duties without constant direction. Thus, they must understand how their parts fit into the whole.

The practices of aligning missions and teaching leadership begin the process of creating leadership magic. They clarify the organization's commitment to accomplishing more than the minimum, and to demanding the best from its members.

ALIGN MISSIONS

*Align the missions of people and the organi-
zation so that the success of one enhances the
success of the other.*

UNDERSTAND MISSIONS
DEFINE AN ORGANIZATIONAL MISSION
DISCOVER A PERSONAL MISSION
CREATE WIN-WIN RELATIONSHIPS
CHOOSE IN OR CHOOSE OUT

UNDERSTAND MISSIONS

I DON'T KNOW WHAT YOUR DESTINY WILL BE,
BUT ONE THING I DO KNOW: THE ONLY ONES
AMONG YOU WHO WILL BE REALLY HAPPY
ARE THOSE WHO HAVE SOUGHT AND
FOUND HOW TO SERVE.

ALBERT SCHWEITZER

Missions reveal purpose. They tell the world what motivates and directs a person, as well as what drives an organization and guides its overall strategy. The mission describes one's relationship with the world by asking how a person or organization contributes to the greater good. Often, missions are described as statements that focus only on how organizations serve customers or the community. Few organizations are so bold as to link their success to the health and vitality of the rest of the world; yet, by establishing this link, organizations can tap a deeper energy source that inspires people in and out of the organization to greater performance. A mission remains constant over long periods of time because it is guided by an inspiring vision of how the world can be. It changes only when the core purpose of its owner shifts significantly. An effective mission is so grandiose that it could take a lifetime to fulfill. Like infinity, it leaves room for continual growth.

Whereas goals and objectives tend to provide short-term direction, missions inform the very basis for existence. Goals and objectives are tactical. When someone meets a deadline or crosses an item off a task list, he or she has met an objective. Taken together, the many objectives and goals that define our lives ideally reflect our missions. Even as the tasks change, the mission that guides them remains constant. Consider some examples of missions:

MY/OUR MISSION IS...

➤ *To facilitate communication between people in order to create a more peaceful world.*
➤ *To nurture spiritual growth so that people may become self-actualized.*
➤ *To bring joy to the world through music.*
➤ *To promote physical and psychological health and well-being.*
➤ *To teach leadership so that people become more powerful and responsible.*

As organizational missions, these statements might belong respectively to a telecommunications company, religious institution, orchestra or band, hospital, and team. If they were personal missions, they could belong to a facilitator, minister, musician, health teacher, and CEO.

Good leaders create focus by helping their organizations develop and pursue meaningful missions, but many organizations stop there. To inspire leadership magic, some leaders take the mission-making practice even further. First, they compel the people in their organizations to develop personal missions. Then, they invite people to gauge how well their missions align with the organization's mission. Ultimately, leaders then challenge their members to determine whether or not they are good matches for the organization.

DEFINE AN ORGANIZATIONAL MISSION

IF LEADERS ARE GOING TO TAKE US SOMEWHERE WE HAVE
NEVER BEEN BEFORE, CONSTITUENTS OF ALL TYPES DEMAND
THAT THEY HAVE A SENSE OF DIRECTION.

JAMES KOUZES & BARRY POSNER

Some organizations possess a mission that establishes their purpose and guides their strategic direction. If your organization has a mission that truly reflects its purpose, and if this mission is actually used to help leaders prioritize and make decisions, then you may want to skip this section. The next few pages are written for those leaders whose organizations started doing things because an opportunity arose, which, in turn, led to a process that has taken on a life of its own. Suddenly, there exists this organization that isn't quite sure what purpose it serves. Its leaders manage tasks rather than pursuing an ambitious mission that helps fulfill an inspiring vision. This section also might help when organizational missions have grown obsolete or have been placed in a manila folder or on some long-lost disk and forgotten.

So let's assume that you are a leader who wants to help your organization define (or redefine) its mission. If your organization is well-established, then you already perform activities that reflect your mission, even if you have not yet put it into words. If you are in the planning stages of a start-up, then you must build your organization's mission on planned activities. Either way, try these steps with several people from your organization. Select those members whose different perspectives and experiences can ensure a multi-faceted view.

STEPS FOR DEFINING MISSION

1. Assess functions.
2. Assess benefits.
3. Prioritize intentions.
4. Synthesize mission statement.

1. ASSESS FUNCTIONS.

Brainstorm about the major activities that take place in your organization. Don't assess their value at this point; just ask what happens.

2. ASSESS BENEFITS.

Brainstorm about the positive effects of your activities. These are the outcomes of your functions, the "so what" of your activities.

3. PRIORITIZE INTENTIONS.

Rank the desired effects in order of value to both the organization and the people it serves. You may want to ask around to be sure that you judge this step accurately.

4. SYNTHESIZE MISSION STATEMENT.

Weave together a direct statement that synthesizes the most important benefits of your organization. If your list of effects has 20 items, focus on the top two or three.

DEFINING MISSION: AN EXAMPLE

An automobile manufacturer could use this process to identify and prioritize its activities into a concise statement. By staying focused on the big picture rather than getting caught up in listing daily activities, the company can create a succinct, meaningful statement.

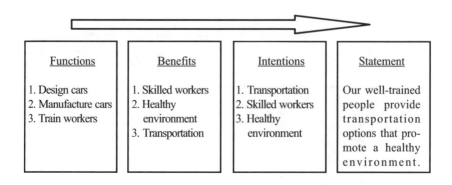

Functions	Benefits	Intentions	Statement
1. Design cars 2. Manufacture cars 3. Train workers	1. Skilled workers 2. Healthy environment 3. Transportation	1. Transportation 2. Skilled workers 3. Healthy environment	Our well-trained people provide transportation options that promote a healthy environment.

While going through this process, you may encounter a few challenges. If it's difficult to distinguish functions from benefits, then focus on value. *Functions* are things people do. *Benefits* reflect the value of those activities. Playing music is a function. Bringing joy is a benefit of that function, a value that arises from playing music. Installing phone lines is a function. Enabling more effective communication could be one of its benefits.

FUNCTIONS & BENEFITS OF ACTIONS

Functions	Benefits
Playing music	Joy
Installing phone lines	Better communication
Leading people	Higher performance
Diagnosing illnesses	Healing others
Managing funds	Creating wealth

If your organization cannot identify two or three essential themes that define a mission, then you may want to invite people from outside your organization such as a supplier or customer to help provide some perspective. They might be able to identify common themes that are hard to see because the themes have been buried by daily tasks. Rather than thinking strategically about their long-term direction, these organizations think tactically about their daily operations. Other organizations have expanded to do so many things or serve so many constituents that they lack any meaningful focus or core purpose. In either case, there is little point in improving performance in an organization that isn't clear about what it does, who it serves, or why.

If an organization possesses two or more distinct components of a mission, prioritize them. Figure out which aspect is the primary driver, which is secondary, and so on. For example, one organization may decide that its primary mission is to increase the wealth of its stockholders, while its secondary mission is to provide excellent health care. When its leaders face a difficult financial management decision, a clear mission will help them make a choice that reflects the organization's priorities. Another company might reverse these priorities, placing excellent health care above shareholder value. So long as those involved with the organization understand its mission, they can then make more appropriate choices.

Most importantly, make sure your organization's mission inspires people! The myriad discussions that can go into defining an organization's mission might compromise any hint of passion. Why create a mission that puts people to sleep? When people inside the organization read the mission, they should feel pride and be motivated to take part in an exciting enterprise. When outsiders hear the mission, it should give them a clear sense of what the organization is about, why it exists, and how it can enrich their lives.

If the organization's mission fails to differentiate it from similar organizations, you must dive back in to figure out what makes the organization special. If you can't find anything that sets your organization apart, your next challenge is to uncover or develop those distinguishing characteristics. As a leader who creates magic, you are responsible for identifying or creating the value that your organization brings to the world. Without value, there can be no magic. Without magic, your group is destined to be less than it could be. If your organization settles for less, the whole world suffers. A mission is that important.

DISCOVER A PERSONAL MISSION

IF THE SUCCESS OR FAILURE OF THIS PLANET,
AND OF HUMAN BEINGS,
DEPENDED ON HOW I AM AND WHAT I DO,
HOW WOULD I BE? WHAT WOULD I DO?

R. BUCKMINSTER FULLER

Every person possesses a personal mission. Some people call it dharma, while others term it fate, God's will, or an inner calling. It's there, whether we recognize it or not and whether we honor it or not. Many people spend their entire lives pursuing it, trying to find that sense of purpose that gives meaning to their lives. Psychologists and spiritual leaders have often decried the despair that can emerge when people lack a sense of meaning. The mission and its pursuit can provide much of that meaning. Leaders cannot claim to know the missions of other people; it's hard enough figuring one out for themselves. Nor can leaders presume to provide people with missions. Those leaders who do so are taking advantage of their authority or power to disempower people rather than empower them. The best that leaders can do is stand in the worthy position of helping others discover their personal missions by creating opportunities for reflection.

Personal missions can be more elusive than organizational ones. Organizations are generally created to meet some need, while people are simply created. Even those who believe that some greater power put us on Earth for a reason must contend with discovering that reason. Either way, personal missions can be identified. No one is born with little manuals that indicate just what that purpose might be. An organization relies on a charter, memo of understanding, or trade association to help define its purpose. You and I must rely on our minds, souls, and intuition to uncover the mission that resides within us. Other people can inspire and support us, but we must look inward to find our own missions.

Some would argue that personal missions are not the concern of organizations. They would maintain that someone's motivations are his or her business alone. To some extent, I agree. It is not the leader's prerogative to pry into the inner desires of group members. Whether a person has joined an organization to get rich, serve others, attain enlightenment, escape reality, or pass the time shouldn't matter to the leader. One who pushes people to share more about their missions than they want to reveal is likely to receive a distorted picture anyway. People will tell such an invasive leader what they think he or she wants to hear.

It is, however, a leader's prerogative to challenge people to know their own missions. A typical leader may not want to be bothered with helping others discover what guides them. However, those concerned with creating leadership magic recognize that people who possess a sense of purpose often perform with greater enthusiasm, consistency, and direction than those who have no conscious purpose.

So, how do you help someone figure out his or her mission? There are several ways. Regardless of how they go about the process, you must begin by explaining why you as a leader are concerned that people be aware of their missions. This can't just be an exercise that people go through because it has been mandated. To truly help people find clarity about their purpose in life, you must keep the focus on their awareness. This means that the exercise can't become a public showcase with people comparing their missions to each other. Comparisons cannot come into play or they will taint the authenticity of the process.

Recognize as well that you do not need people to tell you their missions; indeed, it may be most helpful to have people keep their missions to themselves, especially at first. Doing so may encourage some people to be more honest and bold. Keeping missions private also can minimize people's instinct to tell their bosses, directors, managers, or teachers what they think the leaders expect. Once leaders have clearly communicated the personal nature of discovering a personal mission, they can guide a process that relies on the immediate context or on an inspiring vision.

PERSONAL MISSION: CONTEXT-BASED

One strategy for discovering a personal mission is to use the same technique described above for defining organizational missions. Have a person list what he or she does, not just in the context of the organization, but in consideration of their entire life. Remember that the goal here is to help someone step outside his or her role in the organization and gain a better understanding of his or her life as a whole. The list of activities leads to a list of benefits that the person can prioritize and synthesize.

DISCOVERING A PERSONAL MISSION: CONTEXT-BASED

➢   List activities from personal and professional life.
➢   Identify benefits that derive from them.
➢   Prioritize the benefits.
➢   Synthesize them into a concise statement.

PERSONAL MISSION: VISION-BASED

Other people may discover that they can clarify their missions by first turning to their visions of an ideal world. Though some people use "vision" and "mission" interchangeably, I distinguish them by defining vision as an image of what could be, as an ultimate, idealistic goal of what one wants the world to be, while mission is what someone does in pursuit of that goal.

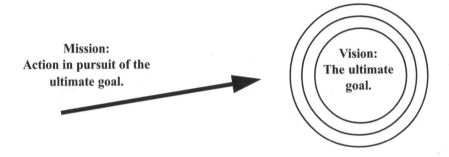

Mission:
Action in pursuit of the
ultimate goal.

Vision:
The ultimate
goal.

Let's say that one person envisions a world in which people of all different races and ethnicities celebrate their holidays together, eat each other's food, and honor each other's traditions. Perhaps by starting there, the person then asks herself what she does to make this kind of a world possible. She recognizes that she often helps build bridges between people of different backgrounds. Sometimes she uses food, other times dance, and occasionally travel. But those are activities. The impact of her activities is that she builds bridges that foster understanding between people. That's what she does. That's her mission.

Some people may not be aware of their idealistic vision of the world. For them, it is important to take some reflective time. They can find clues in their dreams, particularly daydreams. Journaling, meditating, and talking with good friends might be helpful as well. Some people find that guided visualizations help them get a sense of their vision. This process involves having someone create an open-ended story that helps a relaxed person delve inside him or herself to discover an ideal buried in his or her subconscious.

DISCOVERING A PERSONAL MISSION : VISION-BASED

> Identify your vision of an ideal world.
> Consider what you do (or want to be doing) to help create such a world.
> Focus on the impact of your activities.
> Create a succinct statement.

As always, we make sure that our personal missions energize us. Certainly there will be times when we doubt our missions or question their authenticity. They may change as we grow. But we cannot modify them every time we doubt whether they fit us. A mission's role is to help provide people with a consistent purpose. If we alter the mission to reflect our every mood swing, then we miss out on the benefit of discovering a personal mission in the first place.

Leaders do not need to host formal workshops for creating missions. They should encourage and enable people to develop their missions so that they can be used in the next step, that of checking for mission alignment. A leader might do something as simple as ask people to write their personal missions on a note card and bring them to a meeting. They will not have to reveal them. At the meeting, the leader can talk about missions, the organization, and alignment without ever looking at people's cards. A process such as this shows that the leader is more concerned with the intention of the process than with controlling or evaluating people's ability to create a mission. By respecting their privacy, the leader also demonstrates trust in people to take themselves and the process seriously.

When leaders provide the opportunity for discovering personal missions, they offer a tremendous gift to their organizations. It is the gift of trust and caring. Their actions indicate that they are truly invested in the individual's personal and professional success. Such a demonstration can go a long way toward generating magic in the organization. The investment that the leader has made in the individual will likely be rewarded with a similar investment from the individual toward the organization's success. Even in this first practice, the leadership magic has started to build.

CREATE WIN-WIN RELATIONSHIPS

THE BEST WAY TO MOTIVATE OTHER PEOPLE
TO HELP YOU FULFILL YOUR GOALS
IS TO HELP THEM FULFILL THEIR GOALS.

DEEPAK CHOPRA

Leaders make magic by identifying the possibility for win-win relationships between the people and their organization. In each leadership practice, leaders do their best to ensure that both the people and the organization benefit from every activity. Sometimes the rewards are obvious; other times, they are more subtle. One could say that both the people and the organization add value to each other, value that can include—yet generally transcends—measures such as money and time. Leaders check for mission alignment when they understand the relationship between the success of their people and that of their organization. Ideally, such a relationship ensures that personal success is directly proportional to organizational success and vice versa. Each drives the other.

Rather than waiting until a poor match has already been made, leaders relate this win-win orientation to the very purpose of the organization and its members. The organization has a mission. It needs to identify and recruit people who are able to support that mission with the best of their energy and effort. The people have a mission. They seek to join an organization that enables them to manifest their personal mission in the real world, maybe through work, or perhaps through athletic, creative, religious, or other community groups. When the personal and organizational missions align, both parties gain tremendously.

WIN-WIN MISSIONS

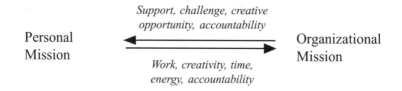

Support, challenge, creative
opportunity, accountability

Personal
Mission

Organizational
Mission

Work, creativity, time,
energy, accountability

Many managers complain that people do not seem committed to the group's mission or vision. Often, they are right. In response, many such leaders develop public relations campaigns to promote their important statements of organizational purpose. They also may redesign reward systems to elicit greater performance. But neither exhorting people through media campaigns nor enticing them with rewards is enough to earn their deepest commitment to the organization's purpose. If people don't believe in the reason for the organization's existence, then it is very difficult to entice them to give the best of which they are capable.

As well, people often complain that they feel unsupported, unappreciated, or underutilized by their organizations. They perceive that their skills and creativity are not tapped to the fullest of their potential. In response, many of them argue that the organization and its leadership are unresponsive to their needs or don't care about them. They might make formal demands to various leaders, or more often, may simply complain amongst themselves about their plight. Neither action is very effective in getting the organization to understand or appreciate the individuals' personal missions.

The only real way for people and organizations to become mutually invested in helping each other fulfill their missions is to align their missions with each other. When missions align, organizations greatly increase the odds that individual actions will serve the organization's needs. A person recognizes that doing things that serve the organization also serves him or her. The conflict between personal and organizational needs has been significantly reduced. People who follow this philosophy are more likely to join organizations that support their personal needs. Going to work (or church, practice, school, etc.) no longer represents a compromise of the person's deeper desires, but a complementary action that fulfills at least a part of that deeper purpose.

Both parties are responsible for checking mission alignment. Before joining or creating an organization, people perform a Personal Mission Alignment Checklist to make sure that the organization would be a good fit. At this point, assume that the person is also checking standard criteria such as rewards (salary or wages, benefits, nonfinancial rewards), time and energy expectations, ability to fulfill responsibilities, status, and personality fit. The mission alignment checklist becomes another important criteria; its level of importance is highly personal.

PERSONAL MISSION ALIGNMENT CHECKLIST

1. Be clear about your personal mission.
2. Find out the organization's mission statement.
3. Secure evidence that the organization's actions are guided by its mission.
4. Assess potential areas for mission conflict.
5. Assess potential areas for mission alignment.
6. Weigh the conflicts and alignments. Compare them to other organizations you could join.

❏   1. Be clear about your personal mission.

Enough said. If you haven't worked out your personal mission, get going. The sooner you establish some clarity about it, the sooner you can use it to make more effective decisions in your life.

❏   2. Find out the organization's mission statement.

Ask different people at multiple levels within the organization about its mission statement. Doing so provides a sense of the actual statement as well as its various interpretations.

❏   3. Secure evidence that the organization's actions are guided by its mission.

Ask internal and external sources for tangible examples of the mission in action. If such examples are hard to find, then you have discovered a major warning about getting involved with an organization whose actions are inconsistent with its stated intentions.

❏   4. Assess potential areas for mission conflict.

Look for ways that the missions could undermine each other. Differences are okay so long as they do not interfere with creating a win-win situation. For example, if your mission centers on providing quality health care regardless of a patient's ability to pay and you're considering joining a hospital primarily driven by maximizing earnings, then you may have an irreconcilable conflict.

❑   5.   Assess potential areas for mission alignment.

Look for ways that the missions can support each other. They do not need to be identical, but the missions should promote a win-win relationship. For example, if your mission centers on providing quality health care regardless of a patient's ability to pay, then you would likely find alignment with a clinic primarily committed to serving homeless people. You might also align well with organizations that provide health education or discounted insurance programs.

❑   6.   Weigh the conflicts and alignments. Compare them to other organizations you could join.

This process is highly personal. There may be a lot of mission conflicts and few alignments, yet joining the organization still could make sense because the needs that would be met are so important. Money can be a very powerful driver here and not just for people in desperate situations. Even if the person's mission and the organization's mission are in profound irreconcilable conflict, the paycheck could be enticing enough to tip the balance. Unfortunately, many people value money over alignment and then can't figure out why they are unhappy. This is a personal call. The obvious win-win would involve finding or creating organizations that best meet a person's total mission, including the financial goals.

People don't have to be new to an organization to follow this process. It can help experienced members clarify how being in the organization serves and does not serve their deeper personal needs. This process prepares them for the choices they face about their commitment to the organization. They should be careful to distinguish their personal mission from their job responsibilities. Just because someone is a marketing director for a telecommunications company does not mean that his or her personal mission is to promote awareness of communications options. A pizza delivery person's mission probably is not to feed the world. Their personal missions likely relate more to the impact they have on colleagues, the quality with which they perform their tasks, or the value they add to their organizations.

Organizations perform a mission alignment checklist as well, one that reflects the same order and priorities as the personal checklist. Obviously, the organization would consider many levels of fit before inviting people to join the organization, promoting them, or perhaps retaining them. The process is highly individualized for organizations as well, since each situation may call for different assessments and weights.

ORGANIZATIONAL MISSION ALIGNMENT CHECKLIST

1. Be clear about your organizational mission.
2. Find out the person's mission statement.
3. Secure evidence that person's actions are guided by his or her mission.
4. Assess potential areas for mission conflict.
5. Assess potential areas for mission alignment.
6. Weigh the conflicts and alignments. Compare to other people you could choose.

☐   1. Be clear about your organizational mission.

Know the essential elements of your organization's long-term purpose, not just the immediate factors that pressure you to invite someone into your organization.

☐   2. Find out the person's mission statement.

Ask point-blank. What drives you? What motivates you? What's your greater purpose? What's your personal mission?

❑   3.   Secure evidence that person's actions are guided by his or her mission.

Ask the person and his or her references for specific examples of behavior that reflects the mission. Also ask references what the person's priorities seem to be.

❑   4.   Assess potential areas for mission conflict.

As a leader, you are responsible for assessing the potential conflicts that could undermine the organization. Will this person fit into the organization culture? What will the person have to compromise in order to fit? Is that likely to occur? What potential negative impact could the person have on the culture?

❑   5.   Assess potential areas for mission alignment.

See how the missions support each other. You are searching for a win-win relationship and cannot compromise the organization in an effort to get it. This is not the time to be revising the organization's mission in order to lure someone into the organization. Look for the gifts that the person would bring to the organization's mission, not just to its daily tasks and objectives.

❑   6.   Weigh the conflicts and alignments. Compare to other people you could choose.

Basically, treat mission as you would any other selection criteria such as technical skill, work experience, or personality. Figure out how well the person would fit within the organization. Then determine the ability of your organization to bring out the best in the person.

Like most good leadership practices, aligning missions happens in the context of regular organization activities. Most information about a person's mission can be gathered during the recruitment and interview process. Most information about the organization's mission can be communicated at the same time. This communication should happen in an explicit manner. The leader should not hesitate to ask questions about the person's mission and to emphasize the organization's mission.

It is equally important to ask people who have been in the organization for awhile check the alignment of their missions as well. Perhaps a teacher started working in a school because both were committed to serving children's academic needs, yet now one or the other has, over time, changed that commitment. By having people occasionally check their personal missions, the leader gives them a chance to get reenergized about their higher purpose. If the daily routine has dulled people's enthusiasm, reviewing their missions may remind them of their deeper intentions. If daily pressure has put them into a reactionary mode, revisiting their missions may help them become more proactive again.

Consider the following examples of people applying for health care positions. The column on the left provides some personal missions, while the one on the right reveals the missions of three different hypothetical clinics. You can see how the examples align with those listed across from each other, yet conflict with the other two.

ALIGNING MISSIONS: A HEALTH CARE EXAMPLE

Health Provider Missions

Clinic Missions

I am committed to ensuring that disenfranchised people have access to safe and competent medical care.

We provide high-quality, critical health care to all community members regardless of their ability to pay.

With patience, compassion, and skill, I help injured people recover their physical and psychological abilities.

Our specially trained therapists enable people who have experienced severe trauma to become more independent.

I believe that by helping people shape their appearance, I enable them to live healthier and more fulfilling lives.

We offer a range of plastic surgery options to help people heal from accidents and surgery or simply to improve the quality of their lives.

Aligned Missions: Excellent fit between the person and the organization.

Almost Aligned Missions: Potential fit between the person and the organization. Further conversation necessary to clarify relationship.

Conflicting Missions: The person's mission conflicts with the clinic's, leading to potentially irreconcilable disagreements related to different priorities.

Like many leadership processes, aligning missions relies on common sense. Unfortunately, few leaders have made it a habit to challenge people to understand *why* they want to join or stay involved with an organization, and few people have had the opportunity to gain clarity on how an organization serves their long-term life's purpose. More temporal—and equally valid—concerns such as money, skill, and experience often take precedence. Checking for mission alignment is an essential selection criteria and sets the stage for making a commitment.

CHOOSE IN OR CHOOSE OUT

IF YOU DON'T MAKE A TOTAL COMMITMENT TO WHATEVER YOU'RE DOING, THEN YOU START LOOKING TO BAIL OUT THE FIRST TIME THE BOAT STARTS LEAKING. IT'S TOUGH ENOUGH GETTING THAT BOAT TO SHORE WITH EVERYBODY ROWING, LET ALONE WHEN A GUY STANDS UP AND STARTS PUTTING HIS LIFE JACKET ON.

LOU HOLTZ

At some point, aligning missions comes down to making a choice. Perhaps a person is considering joining an organization. Maybe an organization is deciding whether or not to promote someone. There are two essential choices faced by both the organization and the person:

1. Choose in.
2. Choose out.

There is no fence-sitting in this process. A person commits to being a part of an organization or not. An organization commits to choosing a person or not. Neither the person nor the organization has the option of kind-of, sort-of, regretfully accepting the other. Making such a half-hearted decision quickly destroys any potential for creating organizational magic.

Magic relies on people recognizing that they have the power to make decisions in their lives. Where they work, pray, play, learn, or otherwise interact with people should be a careful choice. Obviously, there are many factors that each person considers when joining an organization. A key lesson of aligning missions is that we are responsible for making a conscious choice that supports both the personal and organizational missions.

Choosing in means that a person accepts joining an organization, getting promoted, or recommitting to the same position. For the organization, it means that it has invited a person to join it, take on a new position, or continue in a current position.

CHOOSING IN

➢ The person accepts the organization.
➢ The organization accepts the person.

Choosing in establishes a commitment between the organization and the person, but only when both parties have made that choice. When they have, they move beyond simply signing a contract or accepting a job. Choosing in means that the person and the organization have committed to supporting each other's missions. They are not simply performing work or completing a task, for the level of the relationship has been intensified. Rather than only connecting on an operational level, the person and the organization have connected at a purposeful level. If I join your organization, it is not just to complete a few tasks; it is to help you fulfill your mission. This distinction sets a much higher energetic commitment. It invites greater effort because I am supporting your organization's very existence, not just doing routine work.

Choosing in becomes all the more important when people work with an organization on a project or short-term basis because they cannot wait for a close, mutually beneficial relationship to emerge over time. Each party needs the other to give its best from the beginning. I might work for you for only one week, but if both of us have chosen in, then you can be more sure that I will do my best work on your behalf, just as I can be more certain that working with you will support my personal mission.

When an organization chooses to accept a person, the leader can enhance the process by taking the following actions:

TIPS FOR CHOOSING IN:
WHEN AN ORGANIZATION COMMITS TO A PERSON

- ➢ Explain why this person is special.
- ➢ Convey relevant information.
- ➢ Freely give choice.
- ➢ Think calmly and stay grounded.

EXPLAIN WHY THIS PERSON IS SPECIAL.

Explain why you have chosen the person. Clearly articulate the value that you believe the person brings or could bring to the organization.

CONVEY RELEVANT INFORMATION.

Convey any information that the person would need to know before he or she chooses in. Make sure he or she understands expectations, responsibilities, authority, and other essential elements of choosing in.

FREELY GIVE CHOICE.

Do not pressure someone unreasonably into choosing in. Sometimes leaders think that they know what people need and try to control their decision-making process, while other times, they become so focused on the organization's needs that they forget about the person's mission and push the person to make a potentially unhealthy choice. Truly leave the choice in the person's hands.

THINK CALMLY AND STAY GROUNDED.

The organization or person may be under tremendous pressure to make a choice. Nonetheless, act and think as if there were no pressure, as if you had all the time in the world to make the decision. While you know you have a timeline to meet, freeing yourself from a sense of desperation can help minimize the chance that you choose in to the wrong relationship. Do not choose from a place of fear, but from a place of well-reasoned certainty.

The following story offers an example of how one voluntary community organization created a choosing ritual that enabled members to decide whether or not to stay committed. The process could be used in work organizations as well, provided that people have a safe, trusting environment in which issues can be shared honestly. If this environment does not yet exist, individuals still can put themselves through a similar exercise.

WHEN PEOPLE COMMIT TO AN ORGANIZATION

The organization conducted a formal recommitment process every year. No matter how well things were going, each member ceremoniously "quit" the organization, explaining all of the reasons why participation in the group no longer aligned with his or her personal mission. Some of these reasons reflected personal changes while others concerned organizational issues.

Then, no matter how poorly things were going, each member described how being in the group served his or her personal mission. The process raised many important issues. Several meetings over several weeks were necessary to properly address concerns raised during the process of "quitting" the group. The members had to clarify their different perceptions of commitment so that their expectations of themselves and each other were explicit and consistent.

They could then recommit to the organization by expressing the desired terms and conditions of their mem-

bership, or they could choose to move on. Those who did not recommit to the group were honored in their leaving. Their contributions were acknowledged, and their relationships with others in the group were celebrated. Those who recommitted to the group explained why they had done so, which helped the group move forward with renewed energy.

CHOOSING OUT

An essential element of the previous story is that people who left the group were honored in their leaving. Had they been rejected, alienated, or maligned for choosing out, then the process would never have worked. Who can voluntarily recommit to the organization when they anticipate being "punished" for not recommitting?

While choosing in ensures that both the organization and people are committed to each other, choosing out provides a clear strategy for *not* committing to each other. It enables a person to say, "This organization (or this position) does not enable me to fulfill my personal mission, and I cannot be a part of it." It also allows the organization to say, "This person no longer fulfills our mission, and we cannot commit to him or her."

Choosing out requires far more than firing, releasing, quitting, not hiring, or otherwise rejecting a person or organization. It's not just about collecting that last paycheck or receiving a rejection notice. To help people or organizations choose out, leaders develop processes that enable people to leave an organization so that both parties maintain their dignity and integrity. The following story considers a situation in which the leader had to transcend her frustration with someone so that she could create a constructive way for someone to leave the organization.

LEAVING WITH DIGNITY

An organization was having a hard time with one of its managers. The person had worked in a bureaucratic organization that demanded little accountability or innovation. He had lower standards of professionalism than the company needed. After three months of encouraging, supporting, and pleading with him to accept the responsibilities of his position, everyone involved realized that this was a poor match. The organization needed to find a way to let him go without inviting litigation.

One particularly adept leader took a powerful approach. She asked the manager's supervisor what kinds of things the man needed to hear so that he would feel comfortable leaving voluntarily. The supervisor remarked that the manager probably wanted to leave with dignity, assurance of future employability, and financial security to accommodate the transition.

In a matter of days, the organization put together a very realistic plan that enabled the manager to choose out on his own. It hadn't taken him long to make the choice either, since deep down, he also knew that they made a poor match. More importantly, from the leader's perspective, the organization was able to meet its long-term needs and do so in a manner that did not threaten its short-term position. In the end, both the organization and the member made choices in their best interests, and both were appropriately rewarded.

When a person leaves an organization, leaders can do many things to maximize the value of the choosing out and to minimize potentially negative repercussions. A leader can make the often-difficult transition easier for everyone involved by helping people leave positively. The people leaving the organization might tell coworkers, current and potential customers, suppliers, members, and observers about the organization and its leadership. Thus, even though they are no longer officially a part of the organization, they still can affect it. Recognizing this, the leader has a vested interest in enabling people to leave as positively as possible.

Perhaps even more importantly, enabling people to leave well promotes goodwill amongst those who have stayed, including the leaders who dealt with the situation. Approaching transitions with grace distinguishes respectful and respectable leaders from those who would rather preserve animosity.

ALIGN MISSIONS

EXECUTIVE SUMMARY

IF YOU ARE LUCKY ENOUGH TO FIND A WAY OF LIFE YOU LOVE,
YOU HAVE TO FIND THE COURAGE TO LIVE IT.

JOHN IRVING

Leaders inspire organizational magic when they challenge their people and organizations to create, align, and commit to their missions. By helping people tap into their deeper purposes, leaders motivate them to move beyond simply completing tasks and responsibilities. Because they are driven by a mission and not just by a task list, many people rise to a higher level of performance, drawing upon more of their creativity, energy, and skill than they might otherwise have done.

The leader begins by ensuring that the organization has defined a relevant mission. This statement of purpose should describe generally how an organization goes about pursuing some ideal vision of the world. The vision might come from the hearts of workers, investors, leaders, or founders of organizations. Missions differ from goals and objectives in that they have a long-term focus rather than a short-term one. Missions that inspire excellent performance provide ambitious statements that people can always work toward but never quite achieve. Such a mission reveals that an organization must be constantly improving, a key element of creating leadership magic.

Leaders encourage their people to discover their own missions as well, recognizing that each person also possesses a higher purpose, and that those who are aware of their own can develop relationships with organizations that enable them to grow. While money plays a key role in personal and organizational decision-making, leaders should try not to let it cloud their judgement by rushing into relationships that do not make long-term sense.

Leaders invite magic by creating win-win mission relationships between people and organizations. They recognize that each party may offer valuable gifts to the other and that, by aligning their missions, people and organizations can challenge and support each other to perform at their best.

It is not enough, however, to have missions that line up nicely; people and organizations must consciously choose to be in relationship with each other, to commit to each other's success. Leaders expect people to commit not just to being part of the organization, but to actively supporting the organization's mission. They also recognize that, someday, a person's mission may no longer align with that of the organization. Thus, leaders also create magic by enabling people to choose to leave the organization with dignity. This process of choosing out often receives little attention, though it can have intense ramifications for both the organization and the people involved, if leaving is done poorly.

The practice of aligning missions creates organizational magic by revealing the deepest purposes that motivate people and organizations. By having the mission drive decision-making, strategy development, and performance, leaders inspire people to transcend just getting the job done, and draw upon the best that they have to offer. The organization becomes more than simply a place to do things by becoming a place to fulfill one's essential purpose. This practice comes first because once the energy shift has been made, all other leadership practices have an even greater impact.

FUNCTIONS

- Understand missions.
- Define an organizational mission.
- Discover a personal mission.
- Create win-win relationships.
- Choose in or choose out.

BENEFITS

- Provides long-term direction to the organization
- Provides long-term direction to individuals
- Improves individual commitment to the organization
- Improves the organization's commitment to the person
- Enables people to leave the organization in a more constructive manner

ALIGN MISSIONS

SELF-REFLECTION SURVEY

Circle where you are on the scale. Place a star where you would like to be.

		Never				Always
1.	I am clear about the organization's mission.	1	2	3	4	5
2.	I clearly communicate our mission to others.	1	2	3	4	5
3.	I have an inspiring personal mission.	1	2	3	4	5
4.	I align personal and organizational missions.	1	2	3	4	5
5.	I create processes for people to choose in.	1	2	3	4	5
6.	I create processes for people to choose out.	1	2	3	4	5

OPEN QUESTIONS

Consider, discuss, or write about your thoughts and feelings.

1. If I could find the organization that best aligned with my personal mission, it would be...

2. If I were creating an organization that aligned with my personal mission, it would be...

3. My personal mission conflicts with the organization's mission because...

4. The ways that the organization's mission supports my own are...

TEACH LEADERSHIP

Teach people how to become leaders of their own lives so that they can become leaders of others.

THOSE WHO CAN, TEACH
CREATE REAL LEARNING OPPORTUNITIES
GIVE CONSTRUCTIVE FEEDBACK
STRATEGICALLY ASK QUESTIONS
TEACH LEADERSHIP TO RESISTANT PEOPLE
TRANSFORM DESTRUCTIVE LEADERS

THOSE WHO CAN, TEACH

GO WITH THE PEOPLE. LIVE WITH THEM. LEARN FROM THEM.
LOVE THEM. START WITH WHAT THEY KNOW. BUILD WITH
WHAT THEY HAVE. BUT OF THE BEST LEADERS, WHEN
THE JOB IS DONE, THE TASK ACCOMPLISHED,
THE PEOPLE WILL SAY,
"WE HAVE DONE THIS OURSELVES."

LAO-TZU

To inspire their organizations to greatness, good leaders not only guide people but also teach them leadership skills so that they can lead themselves and help lead the organizations. Teaching leadership reflects a core element of a leader's personal mission and serves as a top priority in the organization's mission. As the people in an organization become more powerful leaders, they contribute to the magic making, ensuring that the organization has many people committed to its mission and capable of fulfilling it.

The finest leadership teachers are themselves excellent students: curious, diligent, and fascinated by the possibility of becoming more capable. They recognize that teaching a skill compels a person to understand it well enough to demonstrate and explain it to others. Teaching leadership thus challenges the leader to deepen his or her skills even as it enables other people to improve their performance. This learning cycle inspires more magic by creating an organizational culture committed to learning. When people consistently explore better ways of fulfilling their missions, they are bound to create a more invigorating and productive organization.

Leadership teachers measure their efficacy not by how much time, energy, or money they dedicate to teaching, but by how well their students learn to be effective leaders. Mark Twain's famous statement that "I never let my schooling interfere with my education" reflects how easy it can be to mistake a teacher teaching for a student learning. Effective teachers focus on the student's abilities and potentials. They avoid generic training regimens and emphasize teaching in a way that draws forth the best in each individual.

Because teachers of all subjects have highly individualized styles, this chapter explores some common principles and practices that facilitate excellent teaching regardless of a leader's unique approach. These elements contribute to the magic that enables people to learn.

CREATE REAL LEARNING OPPORTUNITIES

THE GREATEST GOOD YOU CAN DO FOR ANOTHER
IS NOT JUST TO SHARE YOUR RICHES,
BUT TO REVEAL TO HIM HIS OWN.

BENJAMIN DISRAELI

Many leaders find themselves caught in a challenging bind. They want to teach leadership skills to their organization members, yet recognize that many people require extensive practice to become effective leaders. When leaders who are pressured by lack of time and energy simply start delegating new responsibilities to unprepared people, their organizations are in for difficult journeys. As the sailing metaphor reminds us, simply giving someone the helm does not mean the person can steer the ship.

Though some people have learned leadership skills early in life, many find their first and best learning opportunities in organizations and groups. Fortunately, those same organizations need good leaders. As usual with leadership magic, the relationship between people and organizations can be a win-win one. Organizations provide the learning opportunity that people need to become better leaders, while those in training may possess the leadership potential that organizations must tap in order to thrive.

Still, few organizations can afford to spend significant time or money creating hypothetical leadership training programs. They need people to develop their skills while they fulfill their regular responsibilities. The following story describes a relatively low-risk strategy for teaching an important leadership skill: facilitating an effective staff meeting.

LEARNING TO FACILITATE

Each day, a different team member led the staff meeting. During the first few meetings, the most experienced leaders set a positive tone and modeled an effective process. They demanded that people set aside other personal and business distractions, invited them to actively participate, and honored their contributions. Because they set a consistent, sincere tone, the leaders elicited good participation, which led to more productive meetings.

The meeting process was neatly written out on a board next to the meeting facilitator. The agenda first called for concise reports from project team leaders who shared information that could help the other members make more effective decisions. Team members had placed other agenda items on the board before the meeting, along with an expected time allotment to help the facilitator budget the meeting's time frame. When too many items were listed, the group prioritized them so that the most critical elements were discussed. First, items that could be handled in memos or off-line were removed from the agenda. The meeting concluded with a ritual that energized most people and generated greater group cohesion. (See chapter "Guide Rituals").

The physical layout was chosen consciously to maximize meeting effectiveness. The group determined that even for a team of 35 members, a circle would allow each person to be seen and heard. The circle also included places for the facilitator and the agenda board. The meeting room provided the best available light, temperature, and acoustics.

Having established and modeled an effective tone and process for the meetings, the more experienced leaders invited other group members to step into the facilitator role. Though some of them were comfortable doing so, others benefited from having experienced leaders coach them before the meetings. The experienced leaders also created a calendar for signing up to facilitate. This process let people plan ahead so that they would be prepared to run the meetings, and helped the leaders hold facilitators accountable. Some reluctant members needed more encouragement and support than others. The leaders promised to support them in the meeting should they need assistance.

Over the course of the project, every staff member facilitated at least one meeting. In the process, each became a more effective leader and team member. Having had to focus the meeting and moderate discussions, the members became better able to stay focused and discuss issues as regular meeting participants. As the project evolved, several staff members offered suggestions about how to improve the meetings. Thanks to many of these suggestions, the meeting format continually improved. Even something as mundane as a staff meeting began to have the feel and impact of leadership magic.

The leaders in this example have adopted a four-step strategy that can be applied to many situations to foster a variety of leadership skills. As you review the example described above, you will notice that the leaders first modeled the leadership skill, then gave the students a chance to practice it. Next they evaluated the process to refine it. Each step helped the group develop a more effective staff meeting while also challenging the group members to develop their personal skill base.

A FOUR-STEP TEACHING STRATEGY

➢ Model the skill.
➢ Create a real practice opportunity.
➢ Evaluate performance.
➢ Refine the process.

By following this strategy, leaders help people develop their leadership skills while improving the quality of the organization. It's easier to learn under authentic conditions. Educator Margaret Metzger teaches aspiring teachers the difference between real school and play school. The former addresses relevant topics and skills, while the latter just goes through the motions of preparing people for life. Organizations are no different. They can teach based on the reality their people face or simply can pretend to teach them. The leader determines which course to take.

GIVE CONSTRUCTIVE FEEDBACK

THERE IS ONLY ONE THING MORE POWERFUL
THAN LEARNING FROM EXPERIENCE,
AND THAT IS NOT LEARNING FROM EXPERIENCE.

ARCHIBALD MACLEISH

Leaders who effectively give constructive feedback empower people to learn from the mistakes that they inevitably make when practicing their skills. Those leaders who are heavy-handed, vindictive, or contradictory can squelch a person's willingness to learn and minimize his or her ability to do so. Those who fail to give any feedback send the signal that everything is okay. They can be certain that mistakes will be repeated over and over again. As with other leadership skills, no single script exists for offering feedback. However, the following guidelines can increase the likelihood that their feedback will translate into desired changes.

GUIDELINES FOR GIVING FEEDBACK

1. Good feedback comes from a place of caring.
2. Good feedback is constructive.
3. Good feedback holds people accountable for their growth.
4. Good feedback is offered at an appropriate time and place.
5. Good feedback focuses on the essentials.

---

1. GOOD FEEDBACK COMES FROM A PLACE OF CARING.

To create magic, a leader must care about the personal or professional growth of the person receiving the feedback; otherwise it will be difficult to frame the feedback in a way that enables the person to move forward. People can sense when someone cares about them. They are far more likely to open themselves to criticism when the person giving it is genuinely invested in their well-being. Anything less turns the feedback into a mechanical exercise devoid of feeling. Caring focuses the leader on framing the feedback constructively. It says in effect, "Because I value your growth, I am willing to be honest and direct with you." Magic cannot happen between people who do not care about each other.

2. GOOD FEEDBACK IS CONSTRUCTIVE.

Constructive feedback enables a person to move forward by learning from what did not work in the past. It provides specific guidance so that a person can achieve better results next time. It also describes why the change is necessary so that a person understands the intention of the comment. Feedback should never be strictly punitive or used to shame a person. Such a negative tactic might cause some short-term changes in behavior, but they will build resentment that can undermine the organization's dynamics over time. Leaders abuse their power when giving feedback in this destructive way.

FEEDBACK EXAMPLE

(Feedback for a chronically late person)

Destructive: *You're late again! What's your problem?*
Constructive: *We need you to arrive at our meetings on time so that you can help plan our activities. Can you do that?*

Even high-caliber individuals benefit from feedback that helps them more finely hone their skills so that they can improve on their success. Leaders who want their organizations to be the best possible, and not just better than others, constantly search for even the smallest potential refinements.

3. GOOD FEEDBACK HOLDS PEOPLE ACCOUNTABLE FOR THEIR GROWTH.

Nurturing leaders run the risk of over-extending the help they offer people. They might become so eager to see people succeed that they do the work for people instead of in support of them. While well-intentioned, these leaders end up taking away the people's power. Note how the example of constructive feedback presented above ends with a simple question, "Can you do that?" The question directs responsibility back onto the chronically late person. If the person says, "No," then the leader can choose an appropriate response. If the person says, "Yes," then the leader may seek assurances of future punctuality. Well-articulated feedback empowers people to more effectively choose their actions.

4. GOOD FEEDBACK IS OFFERED AT AN APPROPRIATE TIME AND PLACE.

Though organizational life can be hectic, leaders should give feedback only when they are prepared and when those receiving feedback are best able to hear it. Doing so may require setting aside a specific time and place that affords some privacy or otherwise minimizes publicity. Giving individual feedback in a public arena rarely works because there are too many distractions. People might be so embarrassed or angry to receive feedback in front of others that they cannot internalize otherwise valuable comments.

Because feedback is so valuable and potentially volatile, good leaders prepare its tone, wording, and presentation with tremendous care. Perhaps the leader writes out comments ahead of time or brainstorms a list of issues before picking just a few on which to concentrate. The leader thinks about how to say things in a way that improves the person's ability to hear the feedback. Doing so by no means guarantees that the receiver of feedback will respond well, but it increases the likelihood that the receiver will be able to grow from the comments. This extra attention to detail is a hallmark of leadership magic. Attending to the nuances of a feedback session is not unlike trimming a sail or tuning an instrument. Subtle adjustments can have a dramatic effect.

5. GOOD FEEDBACK FOCUSES ON THE ESSENTIALS.

Leaders committed to helping people grow rarely provide them with shopping lists of suggested improvements, yet often are in an excellent position to help people focus their energies on improving one or two skills at a time. For example, one leader may decide that it's more important to have a person stop railroading his colleagues than to organize his calendar, while another leader may think exactly the opposite. Either way, the leader determines which behaviors are most in need of improvement and helps the person concentrate on those.

The following story describes one leader's process of refining how his organization gives feedback relying on the guidelines described above.

DEVELOPING A FEEDBACK PROCESS

The leader was frustrated by his organization's performance review procedure and tired of hearing complaints that it seemed capricious. He wanted a process that would provide people greater direction and focus. While refining the process, he kept a list of the organization's objectives by his side to ensure that the new process reflected these objectives. Thus, he weeded out a number of ambiguous review questions and rating systems that were hard to justify to himself, let alone to the group.

Most importantly, he focused the last step of the review procedure on one simple question: What can you do to improve your performance next time? Reviewers were limited to offering two concrete ideas that a person could implement before the next review. Therefore, any time a group member's performance was reviewed, the person received clear direction regarding one or two things that he or she could work on right away. Broad recommendations like "be more organized" or "try harder" were scrapped. The only comments allowed were tangible suggestions such as "Select and begin using a daily planner by the end of this week," or "Have two colleagues proofread any memo or letter before you send it out." This step significantly reduced the number of protests from people receiving reviews and dramatically increased the speed and efficiency with which people improved their skills.

STRATEGICALLY ASK QUESTIONS

ASK THE HARDEST QUESTION.

MARGARET METZGER

To teach leadership well, leaders rely less on telling people what they think the people need to hear and more on asking them the questions that enable them to learn about leadership on their own. Asking the right question at the right time and in the right way is one of the most difficult communication skills, and it requires far more practice than the typical school or job-based training affords. Here, I touch on some key elements of asking questions, enough to drive home its importance and offer a few helpful tips.

CLOSED AND OPEN QUESTIONS

Closed questions are designed to elicit information and generally call for a concise answer. Questions that invite "Yes" or "No" responses are closed, as are those that provide facts rather than analysis. Leaders can ask closed questions to help a person clarify his or her understanding of a situation and thus provide some sense of future direction. In a world so full of information, teaching people how to understand its impact is vital to their leadership development. The following dialogue between Sandra, a team leader, and John, one of the team members, shows how closed questions can quickly provide perspective on a situation.

CLOSED QUESTIONS GET INFORMATION

John: *The customers were really happy with our service.*
Sandra: *How many of them were happy?*
John: *We're not sure exactly.*

Sandra: So how do you know they were happy?
John: None of them complained.

At this point, the leader has posed a couple of closed questions to gather information that delves beneath the surface of the person's original assertion. The leader can now ask some open questions to challenge the person to think more critically about the situation. Open questions generally invite greater analysis and challenge the respondents to exercise their critical thinking skills.

OPEN QUESTIONS PROBE DEEPER

Sandra: How are you going to find out which customers
*   are happy?*
John: We'll ask them.
Sandra: What would you ask them?
John: If they are happy with our service.
Sandra: What else? How can you dig deeper? How could
*   you learn more about what makes them happy?*

In this example, the leader holds the person accountable for thinking. Rather than just taking over responsibility for developing the survey, the leader uses questions that the person to can think about himself, next time. As an added bonus, there will be times when the person's response proves more effective than anything the leader would have come up with alone. Again, the joy and power of teaching leadership is that it can be done in the context of everyday tasks and responsibilities. Over time, teaching leadership becomes second nature, not just for the leader but for the entire organization.

Open questions are powerful because they lack simple "Yes" or "No" answers and demand more than just a factual response. Because they are so challenging, some group members may try to dodge them with an "I don't know." As you can see in the following example, leaders must then reframe the question so that the responsibility for answering remains on the student.

Here are two suggestions for constructing open questions. First, when someone approaches you with a problem she wants you to solve, turn the problem back to her by asking, "What do you think?" This reversal takes the question-asker out of her passive mode and keeps her responsible, not just for solving the problem, but for thinking about it more intensely. She can no longer acquiesce to others but must exercise her own critical thinking skills. Another effective tool is the simple question "Why?" It pushes people to think beyond the obvious. They are compelled to understand the patterns and causes that influence the organization, much as a sailor studies the current's effect on his ship.

In the following scenario, Sandra helps John better understand the situation and see his responsibility in addressing it.

CONSTRUCTING OPEN QUESTIONS

John:	*Sales are dropping! We need to do something.*
Sandra:	*What do you think we should do?*
John:	*I don't know.*
Sandra:	*What do you think is causing the drop?*
John:	*Well, we're facing more competition.*
Sandra:	*True. But let's say that you're a customer. Why would you have stopped using our services?*
John:	*That's easy. We wanted to lower expenses, so we cut quality.*
Sandra:	*Perhaps. What are at least two cost-effective ways that you could find out our customers' needs?*

Good leaders recognize that there are times to ask questions and times when people need specific directions. Often, questions are underutilized, even though holding people responsible for answers to meaningful questions is a powerful way to challenge them to grow in skill and confidence. The leader who invests time and energy asking strategic questions will be well-rewarded as people learn to ask themselves similar questions and, in turn, teach others the art of asking pertinent questions.

RESPONSE STRATEGIES

Leadership magic shows people how to tap into their power so that they can leverage it on behalf of the organization. We can't discuss asking questions without considering how we invite responses, for it is through the response strategy that we invite creativity and excellence. At times, the most difficult aspect of asking a question lies in eliciting a constructive response. Some organizational cultures communicate very quickly, which means that if you don't answer a question immediately, people may think you don't know the answer, aren't paying attention, or don't care. Other people may interject their responses hurriedly to ensure that they get to speak, and so preclude others from contributing at all.

People respond to questions at vastly different rates for varied reasons. Because of their personalities, some people work out complete responses in their heads before they articulate anything. They check for word choice or make sure that they have captured the idea as well as possible. Others might come from cultures that reward patience and contemplation over speed and aggressiveness. After a question is asked, these people might give extra attention to their response to avoid appearing rude or incompetent. Some would argue as well that gender differences and socialization affect response strategies. Of course, all of these variables are subject to numerous individual exceptions.

Leadership teachers create environments that encourage people to respond to important questions. For example, if a senior management team is developing a strategic plan, but only three of the six members answer any of the questions posed by the board, then the team is operating at only 50% efficiency. If in routine staff meetings, the same small group of individuals answer all inquiries, then consider how much potential intelligence is being wasted. When people refrain from answering questions, both the organization and the individuals suffer. The group misses out on the expertise and perspective of the silent members, while everyone present settles for less in themselves than they have to offer. The choice to participate remains up to the individual, though a leader can develop response strategies that dramatically improve the organization simply by taking advantage of human resources that are already present. This whole leadership magic concept is about tapping power in people that already exists.

When developing their response strategies, effective leaders consider *wait time*, which is that pregnant pause after a question has been asked and before it has been answered. Some question-askers immediately accept the first or loudest response. Others wait for five, ten, even fifteen seconds before inviting a response in order to give people time to think and indicate that they have an idea.

The leader controls the wait time by deciding when enough time has elapsed to invite responses. For example, a leader might ask her colleagues, "How can we respond to our main competitor?" At this point, numerous options influence the wait time and quality of the responses. She might do nothing else and simply let people start talking as soon as they have thoughts to share. This strategy encourages spontaneity and can result in quicker resolution, though it may not invite the best ideas. Some other strategies include:

POTENTIAL RESPONSE STRATEGIES

1. *"Take a few minutes to think about it, and then we'll go around and hear everyone's answers."*

    Benefits: Gives time to think; everyone is expected to answer; everyone will be heard.

    Challenges: Could be too time-consuming, especially for large groups.

2. *"Think about it this evening and write up a list of your four strongest ideas. We'll pass those around in tomorrow's meeting."*

    Benefits: More time to think; respondents must articulate their best ideas in writing; everyone's ideas will be shared.

    Challenges: Delays responses by another day; some might lose focus between meetings.

3. *"Let's break into clusters of two or three to share ideas, then each cluster can report to the whole group about its best suggestions."*

    Benefits: Shy members can share ideas in a less intimidating environment; best ideas are pulled forward by clusters.

    Challenges: One person could dominate a cluster; the cluster could edit out good ideas prematurely.

Each response strategy invites different benefits and challenges. The following checklist can help leaders develop their strategies most effectively.

RESPONSE STRATEGY CHECKLIST

❏ Wait time: How long of a pause before accepting answers?
No pause, 10 seconds, one day, etc.

❏ Response mode: How will answers be communicated?
Writing, speaking, brainstorming, etc.

❏ Audience: With whom will answers be shared?
Small groups, large group, leader, themselves, etc.

❏ Quantity: How many answers should people provide?
Any amount, three, your five best, etc.

❏ Quality: How thorough should answers be?
Spontaneous brainstorm, some supporting evidence, well-researched, etc.

Those who create leadership magic thoughtfully choose the response strategy that best enables the group to meet its objectives. Leaders respect the power of questions to challenge people to learn, participate, and contribute their best ideas to the organization.

TEACH LEADERSHIP TO RESISTANT PEOPLE

THE GREATEST ACHIEVEMENT OF THE HUMAN SPIRIT
IS TO LIVE UP TO ONE'S OPPORTUNITIES AND
MAKE THE MOST OF ONES' RESOURCES.

VAUVENARGUES

No matter how well a leader creates a safe and encouraging environment, nearly every organization possesses at least a few members who resist learning about leadership and some who are downright negative. While some organizations may choose to fire or otherwise remove such people from the organization, others may be compelled to keep them for personal, professional, or legal reasons.

In reality, no matter how hard an organization works to choose members who fit its mission, there are times when some members will not want to grow as leaders despite your best efforts. When that is the case, the organization must remain committed to growing leaders and must continue to develop a critical mass of similarly committed individuals who will ultimately define the culture. Organizational magic is only sustainable when critical numbers contribute to its presence.

Leaders who promote magic are slow to give up on people. Though such leaders often need to dedicate time and energy to other priorities, they recognize that successfully helping a resistant person develop the confidence or desire to become a powerful leader can inspire the entire organization to rise to higher levels of performance. Leaders can use some fairly "common sense" tactics to win over resistant students.

First, let the resistant person know how he or she brings or could bring value to the organization. Too often, in the rush of planning and completing tasks, leaders forget to communicate clearly that they see value in people. They may think that simply inviting someone to join the organization demonstrates how much the person is valued. But this is not always enough. Though some individuals can get by with little or no outside validation, for many others such recognition is vital. They need to hear clearly why they are important to the organization. Their need may stem from poor self-confidence or insecurity, but this is not really the leader's primary concern. Clearly communicating an appreciation of someone's value can invite greater effort from the person, which in turn enriches the organization.

Often, those who resist learning about leadership (or anything else for that matter) lack faith in their ability to become effective leaders. When leaders communicate their faith in the insecure people, they can help them overcome their resistance. After all, part of creating magic is believing that change is possible. The leader's faith can serve as a temporary bridge while the person develops his or her confidence. Sometimes, the leader's task is as basic as saying something like, "I know you are capable of helping guide this organization, and I need your help. You have a lot to offer. For example, you..."

The following story shows this direct approach in action.

OVERCOMING "I CAN'T"

A project team member had been saying "I can't," a lot lately, and his work reflected his commitment to not doing well. His responsibilities were completed sloppily and late, if at all. He was distracting other team members and angering them as well. The leader pulled him into her office. She noticed that he seemed anxious. His body language was tight and defensive. Though she felt frustrated by his recent lapses, the leader realized that coming down hard was unlikely to elicit any changes. His colleagues had already made clear their frustration with his performance. She decided to take a different tack.

She started by taking a deep breath and calming her own energy. She knew that, in the heated pace of an ordinary workday, she became less aware of how to say things so that they had the impact she wanted. Next, the leader looked at him for a moment, long enough to connect with him as a human being. She knew that he was in a precarious place, for he was capable of doing the required work and yet wasn't doing it. Perhaps he faced personal or pro-

fessional problems about which she knew nothing. She re-minded herself that she had an opportunity to help him grow and become an asset to the organization.

These few steps made it much easier for her to estab-lish an effective conversation. As they proceeded, she com-municated clearly how important he was to the organiza-tion, yet offered a few examples of his failures. He didn't want to discuss his personal concerns, but did acknowl-edge that he had been distracted. They developed a plan through which she would provide him more guidance and supervision, not in a heavy-handed way, but in a manner that would help him stay focused on his responsibilities. In turn, he committed to addressing his personal issues, so that they would no longer be such a distraction. She also encouraged him to let some of his colleagues know that he had been going through a hard time and was still committed to the group's success. She hoped that doing so would encourage the other members of the team to sup-port him as well.

Though he wasn't explicitly thankful, the leader no-ticed how much more relaxed he was when leaving her office. It was as if a huge burden had been lifted from his shoulders. Clearly, the burden of knowing that he wasn't doing his best also had been weighing on him.

Over the next few days, his performance improved dra-matically. Though not perfect, he was more responsible. Because she checked in with him fairly often, she was able to help him prioritize. Any potential problems were caught before they became too large to handle. She was grateful that he had been willing to step up to her supportive chal-lenge, and told him so. She knew that such a strategy wouldn't work every time or with every person. But in this instance, her time, care, and faith were well-rewarded.

The ethos of leadership magic permeates an organization. By persis-tently striving to teach even resistant members, the leader reveals his or her commitment to drawing excellence from everyone. Sometimes, however, there are people who more profoundly endanger an organization's integrity and success. They go beyond resisting leadership to actually destroying the organization's effectiveness. Again, however, teaching leadership can prove a powerful tool for finding deeply buried gold, even in these people.

TRANSFORM DESTRUCTIVE LEADERS

TRUE CHANGE AND HIGHER HUMAN ADAPTATION
ARE NOT MADE BY RESISTANCE TO THE OLD HABITS.
CHANGE IS NOT A MATTER OF NOT DOING SOMETHING;
IT IS A MATTER OF DOING SOMETHING ELSE.

DA AVABHASA

Some people get their power from destroying what others create. If a resistant person holds himself back from learning leadership, then a destructive one actively prevents the entire organization from performing at its best. They know how to lead others, yet direct them toward destructive ends. They create ways to sabotage a project, interrupt a meeting, or derail a strategy. Even in the most positive organizations, such negative individuals can attract followers through their ability to instill and take advantage of fear in others. These individuals often derive their power from standing in opposition to the organization's leaders. They distract leaders who are trying to guide the organization toward a common end by denying that there can ever truly be a common end.

Many leaders would remove these people from the organization quickly; yet, at times, dismissal is not an option, and the leader must manage the situation as well as possible. Some organizations are bound by contracts and others by their mission to serve even those whom undermine the organization. Unfortunately, some leaders focus so much attention on destructive people that they begin to manage their organizations in response to them. Heavy controls and overly restrictive regulations often come in response to members who take advantage of a leader's trust. Unfortunately, these same mechanisms can destroy the very magic that a leader hopes to invite. So leaders must look for another option.

Leadership teachers choose an alternative strategy. Instead of trying to subdue the power of the destructive person, these leaders help transform that negative energy into constructive energy. Doing so requires that leaders perceive and acknowledge the destructive person's abilities, and then help guide that person toward a more constructive focus.

REVEALING A POWERFUL LEADER

She was a thorn in everybody's side. None of the managers wanted her or her friends on their project teams. Though she was one of the most intelligent people in the organization, the managers had learned quickly that she could cause relentless distraction by arguing every point, performing to bare minimum standards, and bending every rule to fit her whims. When they were firm with her, she retreated into sullen reticence; when they were lax or ignored her, she took advantage of them even more. The small group that followed her was becoming more brazen as well. Getting rid of her altogether offered a last resort, though numerous internal pressures precluded that measure, for the moment.

The leader had little time and little left to lose. He could hardly alienate her any more. One day, he started a casual conversation with by mentioning a problem that he faced in planning an important event for the organization. Though she remained gruff, she seemed curious as well. He outlined a few possibilities, and expressed a desire to have a capable leader such as her take charge. She was unusually quiet, which he took as a good sign. He asked her if she would be willing to head up a small committee of interested people, most of whom not coincidentally were her "followers." They would need to meet tight deadlines

> *and strict criteria. She'd have to work with him. He clearly indicated his faith in her ability, though he knew he would have to be attentive to her actions.*
>
> *There was risk involved since the leader had put his judgment on the line with others within the organization; he had to justify his stance to more than one manager. Still, he felt confident. He had no doubt that she was capable of meeting the expectations and knew that he could disband the committee if its work proved unsatisfactory. He risked losing face, but he also risked gaining a powerful contributor.*
>
> *The strategy worked. She went on to lead the committee far more effectively than he had imagined. Though there were rough spots, the opportunity ultimately proved beneficial for her as well as for the organization. Her experience compelled the organization to reevaluate its structure to take better advantage of the leadership talent inherent in the group.*

Magic really means the ability to transform energy. Sometimes, a leader helps change passivity into activity or cynicism into idealism. Destructive leaders have already demonstrated that they have the power to lead. They have already learned many important leadership skills, even if their approach is more negative or manipulative than what most leaders want in their organizations. Helping them transform the intentions of their leadership can bring the organization tremendous value. As in all learning, the ultimate decision to transform oneself remains with the individual; leaders can only provide opportunity, encouragement, and modeling. Yet, these are powerful offerings, and those who create leadership magic learn to rely on them.

TEACH LEADERSHIP

EXECUTIVE SUMMARY

NO MAN CAN REVEAL TO YOU AUGHT BUT THAT
WHICH ALREADY LIES HALF ASLEEP
IN THE DAWNING OF YOUR KNOWLEDGE.

KAHLIL GIBRAN

Effective leaders approach organizational life as a series of teachable moments. They create an environment conducive to personal and professional growth. While their styles differ, these leaders rely on common practices that hold people accountable for their leadership development. They create real learning opportunities out of the organization's daily tasks both to minimize the resource drain often associated with teaching leadership and to ensure that the skills developed are directly applicable to the organization's needs. These leaders offer constructive feedback that enables people to learn from their mistakes and improve their performance. They ask questions that make people responsible for their own effectiveness and develop response strategies that invite people to give the best that they have to offer.

Leadership teachers take deliberate care when working with resistant members who lack the confidence to see themselves as effective leaders. Leaders serve as a confidence bridge for these people, maintaining faith in them even when they lack faith in themselves. Dealing with destructive leaders is even more challenging, particularly when they cannot be fired or otherwise removed. By tapping into the destructive leader's innate leadership ability, the leader brings the person into a more constructive relationship with the organization.

The practice of teaching leadership creates organizational magic by recognizing the power in every member to contribute to the success of the common mission. Treating people at every level of the organization as if they are capable of being excellent leaders raises everyone's expectations of themselves and each other. Higher expectations challenge people to perform better than they believed possible.

FUNCTIONS
- Create real learning opportunities.
- Give constructive feedback.
- Strategically ask questions.
- Teach leadership to resistant people.
- Transform destructive leaders.

BENEFITS
- Leadership training in the context of regular activities
- Constant refinement of organizational process
- Enhanced learning from mistakes
- Better information gathering
- Increased number and quality of perspectives
- Decreased sabotage and distraction
- Higher expectations = higher performance

TEACH LEADERSHIP

SELF-REFLECTION SURVEY

Circle where you are on the scale. Place a star where you would like to be.

		Never			Always	
1.	I create real learning opportunities.	1	2	3	4	5
2.	I give constructive feedback.	1	2	3	4	5
3.	I plan how I give constructive feedback.	1	2	3	4	5
4.	I ask questions strategically.	1	2	3	4	5
5.	I elicit responses strategically.	1	2	3	4	5
6.	I find creative ways to reach resistant people.	1	2	3	4	5

OPEN QUESTIONS

Consider, discuss, or write about your thoughts and feelings.

1. The leadership skills I am best able to teach are...

2. The best teachers I have ever had reached me by...

3. As a teacher, I most fear...

4. The people who most challenge me as a teacher of leadership are those who...

II PEOPLE

BUILD RELATIONSHIPS
LEVERAGE DIVERSITY

THE WORST SIN AGAINST OUR FELLOW CREATURES
IS NOT TO HATE THEM, BUT TO BE INDIFFERENT TO THEM.
THAT'S THE ESSENCE OF INHUMANITY.

GEORGE BERNARD SHAW

An organization in which people misuse each other drifts like a ship without a crew. No matter how well their maps indicate the way, and regardless of the skill of their captain, the crew cannot lead the ship anywhere. Not trusting each other's motivations, they cannot rely on each other to fulfill their commitments, and, because the ship needs the crew members to coordinate their efforts, the ship drifts aimlessly. To create magic, the leader ensures that people trust each other and value the numerous skills and experiences each brings to the others. Each person is a gift to the ship; the captain's job is to help everyone see that this is so.

The captain knows that she leads a group of human beings, not robots. Her crew is like the other natural forces with which his ship must interact, for both people and nature possess an often unpredictable capacity to bring the ship safely to harbor or to crash it ruthlessly upon dangerous rocks. To lead effectively, she relies upon compassion, care, and empathy to predict and meet the needs of her crew, and in so doing, she teaches them to do the same with each other. She also values the myriad skills that her crew members bring to the ship. Each crew member has sailed different seas on different ships and learned different lessons. The captain recognized long ago that she alone could never possess all of the skill and wisdom necessary to bring the ship home; she depends upon her ability to tap the skill and wisdom of everyone around her.

Once leaders have helped organizations and people identify their purposes, they build trust and leverage diversity to strengthen relationships. These stronger relationships elicit organizational magic by creating an environment in which people feel comfortable to learn from mistakes, take risks, and perform at their best.

BUILD RELATIONSHIPS

*Create an environment in which people invest
in each other's success.*

THE POWER OF RELATIONSHIPS
CARE ABOUT PEOPLE
EMPATHIZE WITH PEOPLE
TRUST PEOPLE

THE POWER OF RELATIONSHIPS

POINT 8:
DRIVE OUT FEAR. CREATE TRUST.
CREATE A CLIMATE FOR INNOVATION.

ONE OF THE 14 POINTS OF W. EDWARDS DEMING

Leaders lead people, not things, buildings, or strategies. Leaders are entrusted with organizing and guiding people, and together they use tools such as money, objects, and ideas to achieve results. Between every two people, there is a relationship. It can be cold and distant, warm and intimate, or anywhere in between. To understand magic, leaders recognize those relationships, and give them the attention they deserve.

Too often, we view relationships as things that just happen or that take care of themselves. Many express sadness when a relationship "just doesn't work out" or "is bad," as if no one contributed to its neglect or failure. In contrast, some people use a model of relationships that places responsibility on both parties to take care of the relationship between them. They view each person and the relationship as three separate entities, each with its own needs.

RELATIONSHIP MODEL

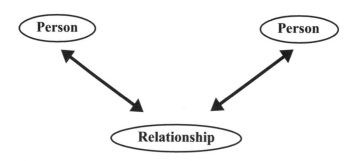

In this model, people are connected to each other through the relationship, and both of them are responsible for meeting the needs of this separate entity. As they take care of the relationship, it enriches their personal or professional lives as well, providing them access to the gifts that other people have to offer. Sometimes a relationship needs time and attention even though both people want to be left alone. Sometimes a relationship needs to resolve a conflict even though neither person wants to do anything about it. If the relationship's needs are not met, it becomes hard and abrasive. Positive energy cannot flow well between the two people because they have not taken care of the entity that connects them to each other.

Imagine how many of these relationships exist in a typical organization—and how many of them get little positive attention. One would not expect a leader to tend to every relationship in the organization, nor could someone actively meet the needs of every relationship of which he or she is a part, particularly in a large group. Yet, at the same time, much of an organization's ability to perform well depends on the health and vitality of these relationships. They are the catalysts for action. If people cannot share ideas, skills, or experiences, they can hardly collaborate well on behalf of the organization.

Leaders who create magic recognize that they cannot control other people's relationships, so instead they create the conditions in which these relationships can grow. By promoting care, empathy, and trust, leaders enable people to take better care of their relationships with each other.

These three key elements nurture relationships so that people can benefit from their interactions. Since many people have grown accustomed to not caring about, empathizing with, or trusting in others, leaders make both their words and their actions demonstrate that their organizations are committed to creating magic through enhancing relationships. All three elements contribute to each other as well. For example, as leaders cultivate more care in an organization, they also contribute to empathy and trust.

RELATIONSHIP SYNERGIES

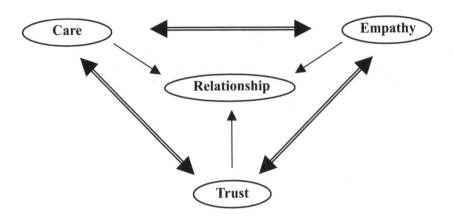

Since most of us want to get along well with others, most people will be eager to follow the leader's example. Will everyone like each other? Probably not. Will everyone want to have healthy relationships with everyone else or be willing to invest the necessary time and energy? Probably not. But they will perform better than they would have in a more adversarial environment, one in which people waste tremendous energy protecting themselves from everyone else.

The next three sections describe strategies for building care, empathy, and trust in an organization. These processes are personal and best taught through example. As with most leadership practices, people learn more effectively and more willingly from observing the skill in action than from being told how to do it.

CARE ABOUT PEOPLE

WE HAVE TO TREAT OTHERS AS PART OF WHO WE ARE RATHER
THAN AS A 'THEM' WITH WHOM
WE ARE IN CONSTANT COMPETITION.

ROBERT BELLAH

The leader who intends to draw forth the very best in people must care about them. Creating organizational magic requires an active and warm heart in addition to intellect and talent. Intelligence is essential, but not enough. Skill is vital, but cannot do it alone. Communication is essential, yet not sufficient. To persuade people that you are committed to their success, you cannot merely pay them well or entertain them with speeches, but must sincerely care about them.

Care comes from within and is revealed through feelings, words, and actions. It demands that leaders open their hearts to the inherent value of those with whom they interact. Leaders who are driven by their position to measure success and performance quantitatively must also develop the ability to measure value qualitatively. Nearly every organization creates performance standards by which it measures the worth of its members. Depending on its needs, an organization may track production levels, billable or volunteer hours, efficiency, or various other categories. These kinds of measurements should continue because they can help the organization attend to its mission. Yet these typical valuation methods do not include the kind of valuation demanded by those who care about people.

Care does not use quantitative measurement, nor can measurement help one care. Opening the heart to other people is a completely different function from most of those that leaders are trained to perform. Caring challenges leaders to step out of often mechanical or routine processes to recognize the inherent beauty of the humanity around them.

VALUING PEOPLE

Measure Their Value   vs.   Care About Them
Track their: See them as inherently
    Productivity   valuable
    Efficiency
    Attendance
    Creativity
    Billable or volunteer hours

Though it can seem like a "soft" leadership skill, the capacity to care might be the most difficult ability for some leaders to develop. It requires courage, confidence, insight, and warmth. As with many leadership functions, caring requires great discipline and concentration, and usually demands them most when conditions are most difficult and leaders are most stressed. Caring is taught in few schools or other organizations. In its place, many people have substituted more objective relationships in which individuals support each other because they are supposed to. Instead of supporting each other because they care about each other, people in organizations often do so out of habit or because of their contracts and job descriptions. While this kind of support still can lead to good organizational performance, its coldness prevents organizational magic. That extra effort comes only when our hearts are engaged in each other's success.

Because our ability to care about others is so intertwined with our personal histories—and perhaps even our genetic programming—it becomes a skill difficult to possess, let alone learn or teach. After all, how do you motivate others to open their hearts to feel compassion for each other? You can't order people to do so, nor can you quantitatively measure the degree to which people have done so.

Rather than give up in the face of such subjectivity, leaders who create magic start with themselves. They commit time and energy developing their own ability to care about people. They approach this process as they would any learning opportunity. First, they set goals; then they find teachers. These teachers—who could be friends, colleagues, therapists, spiritual leaders, family members—can help them overcome the obstacles to caring that they have erected inside themselves.

Like other leadership skills, caring requires practice, and so leaders give themselves the opportunity to exercise care. It may seem strange to set aside time to practice a skill that is so fundamental to living, yet few people have had role models capable of demonstrating their care. Also, the pressures of many organizations can squeeze the ability to care right out of us. Those who care deeply about their families and friends may shut down their feelings when they go to work because it is such a cruelly competitive or dehumanizing place. To open one's heart in such an environment would be absurd. Unfortunately, if people spend 40-50 hours per week in a place that requires them to stop caring, then this detachment and indifference can become a hard habit to break.

The following story describes a leader who no longer liked—let alone cared about—a specific person in his organization, someone who was creating problems because of her carelessness and disrespect. He had tried the standard positive and negative incentive systems, unsuccessfully using both the carrot and the stick to try to change her behavior. He didn't have the authority to get rid of her and so was forced to seek an alternative.

THE KEY OF CARING

The leader lay awake at night—again—thinking about that person who had been driving him crazy at work. She wouldn't follow his directions or complete projects to his specifications. Her defiance was offensive and frustrating. He wished he had the authority to get rid or her.

The next day during a staff meeting, he looked over at her and felt his anger burning inside of him. He had grown accustomed to this feeling. The burning filled nearly his whole body. Though he was supposed to facilitate the meeting, she kept distracting him every time she rolled her eyes or made a cynical comment. The group had been doing fine, but the leader knew that this woman was not contrib-

uting nearly what she could, and her behavior was keeping him from being very effective. He just didn't have the time or energy to deal with her behavior. There were too many other responsibilities to contend with.

The next night, something clicked. He realized that he did not care at all about the woman's success. His anger had grown to such an extent that it completely overshadowed any value she might have. Though he had tried to hide his disdain for her, he was certain she could sense it through his voice and body language. At some level, she knew he didn't care.

Over the next few days, the leader softened his anger toward the woman. He tried to look beneath the surface of her behavior and figure out why she was acting this way. He certainly couldn't psychoanalyze her, nor would he want to. Finally, he looked past her behavior and even past the many possible reasons for it. He just looked at her as another human being, doing what she could to get by in life.

Reaching this base point helped the leader tremendously. He spoke with the woman differently, checked on her performance with less detachment, and was able to thank her for her few contributions with greater sincerity. He even started looking her in the eyes again, something he had not done for some time. There was no drastic miracle, but in time, the woman became less and less obtrusive. Though they were still far from best friends, the leader found a way to connect with the woman that enabled them to support each other's performance.

The best way to teach caring is by example. The more a leader cares about others, the more he shows them the value of caring. As he contributes to their sense of well-being, they have more energy and willingness to do the same for each other.

SYNERGY OF CARING: PART 1

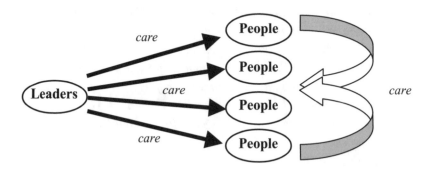

I strongly discourage leaders from adopting the word "caring" as a mantra that gets woven into every speech and document. Doing so can minimize its value and make people skeptical about the leaders' sincerity. If they want members of their organizations to care about each other, leaders should care about them. Walk the walk. When leaders make caring a priority in their lives, their people are more likely to do so with each other.

As people care more and more about each other, they are better able to care about the customers, suppliers, investors, partners, and other community members who interact with the organization. When they care about these other constituents, they better ensure that the needs of these parties are met. The ripple effect can be profound.

SYNERGY OF CARING: PART 2

Leaders who care do not let this feeling cloud their judgment. Caring does not replace performance expectations or responsibilities, but complements them. All else being equal, a leader who cares about people will elicit greater performance from them than a leader who does not.

EMPATHIZE WITH PEOPLE

IT IS THE INDIVIDUAL WHO IS NOT INTERESTED IN HIS FELLOW MEN WHO HAS THE GREATEST DIFFICULTIES IN LIFE AND PROVIDES THE GREATEST INJURY TO OTHERS.

ALFRED ADLER

Empathy is the capacity to share in another person's feelings. Empathic leaders can step outside themselves and climb into the skin of someone else so that they better understand what life might be like from that person's perspective. It is not the same as sympathy, which means that a person feels the same as someone else does. Empathy means that you must share an awareness of someone's feelings.

SYMPATHY VS. EMPATHY	
Sympathy You are sad. = I am sad.	Empathy You are sad. = I am aware that you are sad.
You are angry. = I am angry.	You are angry. = I can understand why you are angry.

Mature leaders have the capacity to look beyond their own responsibilities, perceptions, and feelings, so that they can recognize those of others. They are not selfish. They can anticipate what is happening with other people in the organization because they pay attention to those people's needs, behaviors, and words. Much of this observation can happen discreetly rather than through official surveys and meetings. While formal strategies for finding out what is happening have their place, leading with empathy most reveals itself informally through how one connects with others.

The empathic organization reveals its power when people come under tremendous pressure. When they are in crisis mode, non-empathic organizations can often be identified by the way their members take out resentment of the crisis on each other. Because everyone is so focused on personal agendas and so afraid of what is happening, they cannot look outside themselves to realize that everyone else is in the same boat. In empathic organizations, people are more likely to turn to each other for offering and soliciting support to overcome the problem. These groups of people do not turn against each other when things get difficult, but reach out to each other to leverage their resources.

Leaders teach empathy by practicing it with people. When an employee has made a mistake because he or she is overwhelmed, the leader can say something like, "I imagine that it's challenging being the new kid on the block. Is there anything I can do to support you?" Such a simple gesture acknowledges the person's situation and opens the door for potential constructive action. In other circumstances, a leader may not even say anything, but might place a flower or cup of coffee or funny comic strip on the person's desk as a gesture of connection.

Like care, empathy is a skill that one cultivates internally and which can be difficult to develop because of complex psychological or emotional issues. As leaders develop empathy in themselves and in others, some helpful questions can smooth the path. In asking these questions about a situation, people compel themselves to step outside of their own experience and into that of someone else.

EMPATHY QUESTIONS

How might he feel right now?

What might she think about what just happened?

What might this problem look like from his perspective?

What might she need or want right now? Tomorrow? Next week?

These empathy questions are very different from asking, "What would I do, think, or feel if I were in his shoes?" Empathy is not about what you would do based on *your* experiences, values, or priorities; it is about trying to understand how others might be feeling based on *their* experiences, values, or priorities. These questions also emphasize the word "might" because no matter how empathic a leader is, one can never know exactly how someone feels or precisely what she thinks. Using "might" keeps people honest and reminds them that no one can know with certainty about another person's experience.

Empathy's primary contribution to creating organizational magic is that it challenges us to step outside ourselves to see and understand the humanity in others. Doing so further enables us to respect other people's gifts and challenges. When an organization is doing well, empathy helps nurture relationships. When it faces a serious crisis, empathic people are more likely to cooperate to guide each other and the organization through the situation with as little pain as possible. Empathy is a valuable tool for people committed to working together.

TRUST PEOPLE

LEAP, AND THE NET WILL APPEAR.

JULIA CAMERON

Leaders who guide magical organizations have earned people's trust, including their own. They have created a climate in which people are supported to perform well, grow in their skill base and leadership ability, and pursue their personal mission. These are the leaders who can be counted on, particularly when pressures mount. These leaders have earned people's trust by caring about them, acting on their behalf, and providing consistent guidance. While being trustworthy may seem like an obvious leadership skill, many leaders are not fully trusted by those upon whom they depend and who depend upon them.

Bear in mind that by the time most people join organizations, particularly for work, they may trust others or their leaders only a little. Having been burned in the past by unmet expectations, most people give trust only to those who have earned it. Having also felt burned in the past, leaders are in a similar situation and usually need people to earn their trust rather than freely giving it to them. Nonetheless, one has to start somewhere, or the organization gets trapped in the stalemate of distrust. In organizations committed to performing at their best, leaders must take the first step of earning trust from people. As the leader models trusting and being trustworthy, other people are more likely to follow suit.

GUIDELINES FOR EARNING TRUST

- Be dependable.
- Be ethical.
- Be consistent.
- Be trusting.
- Ask for guidance.
- Give meaningful responsibility.

BE DEPENDABLE.

When leaders make promises, they must keep them. If there is no way to keep a promise, they promptly and clearly explain why. These instances should be rare. If breaking promises becomes a pattern, even the best explanations will lose their impact, and people will not value the leader's commitments.

BE ETHICAL.

If people see a leader cheating others, they will expect the leader to cheat them as well. Because ethics are subjective, leaders establish standards for right and wrong behavior, and people expect them to meet their own standards.

BE CONSISTENT.

If people never know what to expect from the leader's behavior, direction, or ideas, then they cannot trust how the leader will respond to their actions and decisions. Consistency of intention and of action are equally important.

BE TRUSTING.

If leaders guide people by trying to control every decision and action, they appear to distrust people's abilities to make good decisions or take appropriate action. Controlling leaders earn little trust because they trust little. They also imply that other people cannot be counted on, and thus promote distrust between others.

ASK FOR GUIDANCE.

When leaders sincerely ask for guidance and feedback, listen to others' comments, and, if appropriate, implement their suggestions, they signal that they value their contributions. Rather than considering themselves omnipotent beings, these leaders acknowledge that they can benefit from the others' input.

GIVE MEANINGFUL RESPONSIBILITY.

When leaders give meaningful challenges, they indicate faith in others' ability to perform well. This action should not be taken lightly or just as a trust-building exercise; leaders delegate important items because they honestly believe that people can rise to the occasion. Giving someone an important task just so they feel good can be demoralizing to everyone, particularly if the person doesn't possess the skill to be successful.

As with the other elements of leadership magic, building trust happens in the context of everyday operations. While hypothetical trust-building exercises have their place, especially early in a relationship, trust is built most effectively through practical experience.

There are also "quick and dirty" ways to betray trust. These ensure that little magic emerges in the organization. Remember that the energy within a group is transmitted through relationships. When trust is destroyed, those relationships can no longer serve as energy transmitters. No trust, no relationship. No relationship, no energy. No energy, no magic.

STRATEGIES FOR DESTROYING TRUST

- Pretend you trust people.
- Change the rules in the middle of the game, but don't tell people.
- Make important decisions without soliciting input.
- Ridicule people in public.
- Motivate through fear and shame.
- Reward dishonesty.
- Lie, cheat, or steal, even a little bit.
- Fail to provide access to the information or resources necessary for people to succeed.
- Fail to trust yourself.
- Lose control of your rage.

To be trustworthy in the eyes of others, leaders must trust themselves. They don't have to be perfect or completely in control; leaders face enough pressure without pressuring themselves to excel at everything all of the time. Yet the leaders who trust themselves provide a much better model than do those who always second-guess themselves or put themselves down. People need leaders who believe in themselves enough to handle making the occasional mistake gracefully.

A trustworthy leader is better able to help people trust themselves, which is a necessary component of trusting others. There are times when a leader may trust a person even more than the person trusts himself. As a trust builder, she sees his potential strength and gives him opportunities to use it. Along the way, the leader maintains faith in the person, helping him work through insecurities, guiding him along his learning curve.

MAINTAINING FAITH IN A PERSON'S POTENTIAL

He came to the organization quiet, shy, and apologetic. A less magical leader would have allowed or even encouraged him to remain silent and deferential. He was a perfect candidate for being underestimated and overlooked. Yet the leader had seen a spark in his eyes when he mentioned his mission. Though he spoke with little confidence, he had valuable things to say. If he was willing to give up on the "I'm sorrys" and "I don't knows," the leader was certain he could contribute well.

At first, the leader gave him small but visible responsibilities that challenged him to interact often with others in the organization. His tasks were the kind that can get overlooked but ensure that a group operates smoothly. The leader made sure that his role was not overlooked. When he was successful, others honored his achievements. When he made a mistake, or when his confidence faltered, he received encouragement and guidance.

The transformation didn't take long. Within a matter of weeks he became a tremendous asset to the organization. He spoke with fewer and fewer unnecessary qualifications. His responsibilities grew in depth and value. His success had stemmed from his willingness to trust himself and the organization's willingness to trust him. Both components enabled his growth.

As the story above indicates, trust building is a process that deepens over time, yet it does not take as long as many people think. An organization that builds trust into its ethos can help people deepen their trust in themselves and each other in a few hours, days, or weeks. The longer an organization consciously fosters a trusting climate, the deeper their connections grow. Just as some people start saving money early because they recognize the impact of compounded interest, others start building trust early because they know that, like interest, trust grows exponentially.

Whether they use training programs, ropes courses, non-competitive games, or daily tasks, leaders often follow a basic sequence for building trust. First, they start by creating hypothetical situations for building trust. They might use role-playing or exercises like trust falls to give people an opportunity to know each other and begin depending on each other in a relatively low-risk environment. If things don't go well in a role-play, the normal operations of the organization usually aren't affected.

Eventually, however, people need to build trust in a real environment. Some leaders like to challenge groups with big trust exercises right away. They may give a team a very demanding responsibility, figuring that the pressure of the moment can cause people to gel quickly and rally together. While this sink-or-swim method works occasionally, it cannot be counted on to produce trust or, more importantly, good results. One organization that tried the sink-or-swim method with twenty project teams found that those who were successful depended on lucky personality matches, but there were only four such teams. The other sixteen teams became mired in predictable miscommunication, distrust, and confusion.

More effective leaders start by having people work together on more simple, lower-risk tasks, figuring that as they get to know each other better and work out conflicts on small items, they will be better prepared to take on more risky and important tasks. These leaders anticipate that people will grow in confidence in themselves and each other through many small successes. This approach also lets leaders give valuable feedback along the way, guidance that can make a dramatic difference in a group's capacity to succeed. It doesn't have to take long. Many small tasks in a few days can go a long way toward preparing a group for more significant work.

Leaders who try the sink-or-swim method tend to approach group excellence as a random occurrence. They toss people together, give them some responsibilities, then cross their fingers and hope for the best. Those who build trust early have faith in a group's ability to create excellence through hard work, practice, and guidance. Organizations face enough intangibles; they need their leaders to make magic through building trust whenever possible.

BUILD RELATIONSHIPS

EXECUTIVE SUMMARY

...WE NOW REALIZE AS WE HAVE NEVER BEFORE OUR
INTERDEPENDENCE ON EACH OTHER; THAT WE CANNOT
MERELY TAKE, BUT WE MUST BE WILLING TO SACRIFICE
FOR THE GOOD OF A COMMON DISCIPLINE, BECAUSE,
WITHOUT SUCH DISCIPLINE, NO PROGRESS IS MADE,
NO LEADERSHIP BECOMES EFFECTIVE.

FRANKLIN DELANO ROOSEVELT

Leaders inspire organizational magic by creating an environment that respects people and the relationships between them. They do not do this because they are warm fuzzy types or wish to impress others with their sensitivity. They attend to human relationships because they realize that these connections define an organization's ability to become its best. Building relationships is a performance-based strategy that requires leaders to possess courage, discipline, and tenacity.

While intelligence and technical skill serve leaders, their ability to care about people lets them create organizational magic. Care is not an intellectual exercise, but a practice of the heart. A leader who cannot care about people cannot hope to inspire them to do their best. As leaders demonstrate their care for others, members learn from them and begin to care about each other. As they care about each other, the whole organization can care more about customers, suppliers, investors, and anyone else who comes into contact with it.

Once they have stepped outside themselves by caring about people, leaders continue to build relationships by empathizing with them as well. Empathy requires leaders to become aware of how others might feel, think, and perceive. If caring compels leaders to value other people, empathy challenges them to better understand others. As the leader empathizes with them, people empathize with the leader and each other.

Caring and empathy contribute to building trust. Leaders create a climate of trustworthiness in which people can depend on each other for support. Trust should not be given haphazardly by any party, but is earned through common experiences in which people learn to have confidence in each other. The leader creates opportunities for trust building, recognizing that it doesn't have to take long and that, the sooner one starts, the sooner the organization benefits.

Leaders can use care, empathy, and trust to invite organizational magic, yet people must go through their own process of opening themselves to these practices. Many of us have learned to protect ourselves from forming meaningful relationships, particularly in a work environment. Beginning to build such relationships requires a leap of faith—or of trust—from the leader and others. Organizations not willing to take such a leap are destined to be always less than what they could be, while those that take the risk open themselves to the possibility of becoming magical organizations.

FUNCTIONS
- Attend to relationships.
- Care about people.
- Empathize with people.
- Trust people.

BENEFITS
- Better energy flow between people
- Ideas and skills shared more freely
- Stronger cohesion when under intense pressure
- Better relationships with other constituents
- Enhanced ability to see multiple perspectives
- Fewer distractions caused by adversity

BUILD RELATIONSHIPS

SELF-REFLECTION SURVEY

Circle where you are on the scale. Place a star where you would like to be.

		Never				Always
1.	I make building relationships a top priority.	1	2	3	4	5
2.	I care about the people in my organization.	1	2	3	4	5
3.	I let people know that I care about them.	1	2	3	4	5
4.	I empathize with people even if we disagree.	1	2	3	4	5
5.	I am trustworthy.	1	2	3	4	5
6.	I trust other people in my organization.	1	2	3	4	5

OPEN QUESTIONS

Consider, discuss, or write about your thoughts and feelings.

1. For me, the most frightening or frustrating aspects of relationships are…

2. I show people that I care by…

3. I trust myself most when…

4. I trust other people when…

LEVERAGE DIVERSITY

Value and utilize the skills, talents, and perspectives of the organization's unique members.

REDEFINE DIVERSITY
KEEP DIVERSITY PERSONAL
ASSESS COMFORT ZONES

REDEFINE DIVERSITY

IN PROPORTION TO THE DEVELOPMENT OF HIS INDIVIDUALITY,
EACH PERSON BECOMES MORE VALUABLE TO HIMSELF AND
THEREFORE MORE VALUABLE TO OTHERS.

JOHN STUART MILL

Diversity has become a loaded word for many leaders. Upon hearing it, some people think that it means race relations or affirmative action, others start calculating demographics, and still others simply feel paralyzed, afraid they're going to offend someone by saying the wrong thing— whatever that is, this week. Too often, the very mention of diversity in the workplace has bored, angered, and alienated people, causing many leaders to become so cautious when working on diversity issues that they cannot do anything meaningful.

That said, there are still leaders who think of diversity as a trend or distraction rather than as a legitimate leadership concern. They may promote the illusion that people are all the same, possessing the same needs, abilities, and perceptions. They may question why we should address differences when, biologically, we're all similar, anyway. This model works well with machines that have been engineered to consistent specifications. If I am in charge of a fleet of vehicles, I can trust that all of the Ford Econoline vans are going to have essentially similar needs, with some room for individual nuance. After all, they have been made the same way with the same parts perhaps by the same people from the same plant. Henry Ford intended to create a manufacturing process that left little room for variation, and he was successful. Some managers seem to have that same approach to human beings, yet it doesn't work. It never has. Even the most controlling leader in the most regimented organization cannot make diversity go away.

Diversity simply means the existence of difference. People are diverse. It's not a political issue, but a human one. We cannot argue about whether or not diversity is important any more than we can argue about whether or not genetics, or weather, or stars are important. These elements are a part of our world, just as diversity is. Good sailors would never confront the wind or currents by pretending they do not exist, nor would good sailors pay attention to only the loudest currents and breezes. Instead, they learn how to use the keel and position the sails to steady their crafts and propel them forward, accounting for all the nuances nature provides. Similarly, effective leaders learn how to create an organization that takes advantage of the myriad differences of its people, one that leverages this inherent diversity to make their organizations more effective.

KEEP DIVERSITY PERSONAL

WE ARE EACH SO MUCH MORE THAN WHAT SOME
REDUCE TO MEASURING.

KAREN KAISER CLARK

The best way to prevent diversity from becoming a political bombshell is to keep it personal. Leaders who focus on personal issues rather than the latest media-driven trends will be able to develop a strategic approach to leveraging diversity that transcends societal whims. By consistently weaving diversity into the fabric of the organization, leaders avoid being forced to contend with it under pressure because a challenging incident erupts in the community or organization.

Human beings are complex, so leaders broaden their organization's approach to diversity so that it encompasses many elements. Some include:

SOME DIVERSITY ELEMENTS

Learning Styles	Sexual Orientation
Intelligences	Gender
Values	Experiences
Health	Personality Profiles
Physical abilities	Missions
Race and Ethnicity	Family History
Belief Systems	Age
Political Affiliation	Language Skills

Even this partial list clarifies why diversity can be so difficult to manage. Some people lie in wait for the leader to forget to mention a trait that is important to them as proof of the leader's ignorance or cold heart. Tremendous energy can be wasted on these petty conflicts. The resolution of such discussions rarely pleases anybody and certainly doesn't teach anyone anything of value.

By keeping diversity a personal issue, leaders compel people to view each other as individuals, to connect as individuals, and to help each other become more effective as individuals. The following checklist can help leaders gauge how well an organization keeps diversity focussed on personal issues. If any of these questions is answered negatively, then organizational magic is in jeopardy. People cannot give their very best unless they can participate fully. They can do well—they can even perform to very high standards—but in order to achieve their personal best, they need to be comfortable being fully present.

CHECKLIST FOR KEEPING DIVERSITY PERSONAL

❏   Are people talking about their own experiences?

❏   Are people listening to others' experiences?

❏   Are people reaching out to those who may be more reserved?

❏   Are people reaching out to those who may have less in common
     with everyone else?

❏   Does everyone have the opportunity to participate actively?

❏   Is everyone valued for his or her uniqueness?

Keeping diversity personal is more than a "feel-good" exercise. It is a process through which the organization receives the highest value from each of its members. Often, organizations fail to tap the experiences and insights of their members. That's a diversity problem because it means that the leadership has undervalued what people have to offer. By not learning how people can contribute, the leaders don't benefit from their value. Imagine a power plant that didn't use the full capacity of its generators even when the company was failing to meet customer demand, or a military unit that kept its weapons under lock and key even when going into battle. We would look at their leaders, shake our heads, and wonder why they were wasting their resources, especially in a time of intense need. Yet organizations do this all of the time by approaching challenges with little regard for people's unique qualities.

Leaders can create magic by making decisions with diversity in mind. Diversity should rarely be seen as a special event; rather, it should be considered in the context of everyday activities. While each organization faces unique circumstances, here are some general examples of how leaders can leverage diversity to elicit the best participation from their people.

STRATEGIES FOR LEVERAGING DIVERSITY

➢ Communicate through different modalities.
➢ Value experiences.
➢ Create diverse teams.

COMMUNICATE THROUGH DIFFERENT MODALITIES.

People gather information through many avenues. Memos, verbal cues, and visual diagrams impact them differently. Leaders recognize that people communicate in various ways and so provide numerous avenues through which they can get the message. Some would best learn about a new manufacturing process by reading about it, others would want to see it in action, and still others would need to actually perform the process to understand it.

VALUE EXPERIENCES.

People come to organizations carrying a set of lessons learned from other experiences. By providing avenues for them to share those experiences, leaders ensure that the organization benefits most from the collective experience on hand. Rather than seeing new participants as liabilities because they have to be retrained or acculturated, effective leaders enable people to bring the best of what they have learned to their organizations.

CREATE DIVERSE TEAMS.

While they can be challenging to manage, diverse problem-solving teams maximize the development of a broad range of potential solutions. The benefits of having a diverse team are obvious when men and women work together to address designing restrooms in a stadium, when a multi-racial group considers how to market a product in various communities, or when an intergenerational group develops a religious ceremony. Any well-coordinated, diverse team adds value simply by expanding the boxes in which people think.

As with all other leadership skills, leaders teach best by being consistent role models. Leaders should let the organization know how they approach diversity and whether or not they are using an inclusive, personal model such as the one described here, or one that is more limited. When leaders learn from those who are different than they are, or form explicitly diverse teams around themselves, they communicate the value they place on leveraging diversity. When leaders teach people how to communicate according to different modalities, they enable people to see the direct link between performance and diversity. Diversity, which was once seen as a problematic public relations or human resources issue, quickly becomes a strategic tool for creating organizational magic.

ASSESS COMFORT ZONES

IT TAKES COURAGE TO LEAD A LIFE. ANY LIFE.

ERICA JONG

A leader can talk and talk about the value of diversity, and yet people may withhold their contributions. A leader can reach out to all kinds of people to demonstrate how powerful leveraging diversity can be, and yet they may be reluctant to follow suit. Although a leader has the courage or confidence to take some of these risks, others in the organization may not feel so secure.

Some leaders are content to leave the situation as it is. After all, they reason, you can't force someone to feel comfortable participating more fully in the organization. In one regard they are right: a leader cannot order people to participate any more than a leader can motivate them by ordering them to care, or teach them by ordering them to learn. But a leader would be negligent to let people withhold their contributions and fail to learn from the potential contributions of others.

I have developed the Comfort Zones Model to provide leaders with a tool that encourages people to look at diversity first as a personal experience so that they can then make it a more positive organizational experience. As with all of the practices in this book, the ultimate goal of leveraging diversity is to bring out the best individual and group performance. Only through excellent individual performance can an organization become its best. The philosophical approach that supports Comfort Zones is grounded in my ten years' experience as an educator and promoter of diversity. The philosophy itself can be valuable as leaders develop techniques for incorporating diversity more effectively into their strategic decision-making.

THE COMFORT ZONES PHILOSOPHY

1. People perform best when they continually improve.
2. People continually improve when they have opportunities to learn.
3. People learn best when they feel comfortable participating fully.
4. People participate most fully when they do not feel compelled to withhold parts of themselves.
5. People do feel less compelled to withhold themselves when they know that they are valued.

Corollary: People who feel valued are better able to value others.

The leader who acts on this philosophy creates a powerful cycle. To improve how a person performs, a leader starts by helping the person feel valued. How could a leader demand that people perform at their best when the people do not believe they are able to do so? People can only perform as well as they believe they can. That doesn't mean that faith in themselves sets the minimum, but that it sets the maximum of that which they can achieve.

To help people organize their feelings and perceptions, Comfort Zones are organized into four areas like a target: Very comfortable, Mostly comfortable, Not-so comfortable, and Not comfortable. People can mark where they fit and where they think others fit within these areas.

COMFORT ZONES TARGET

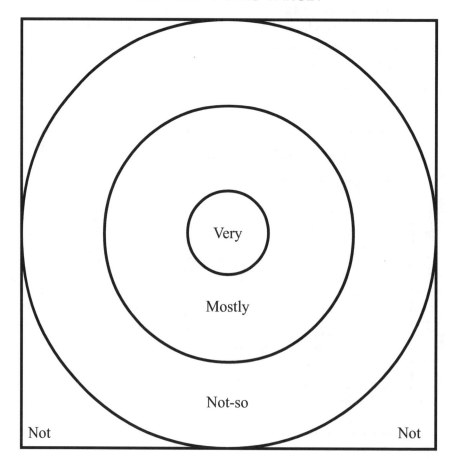

© 1999 Ben Valore-Caplan

COMFORT ZONES CATEGORIES

VERY COMFORTABLE

This organization feels great. I can be myself here without holding back. People respect me for who I am, and I can do my best.

MOSTLY COMFORTABLE

This organization works well for me most of the time. Though I hold back somewhat, most of my colleagues respect me for who I am, most of the time. I perform close to my personal best.

NOT-SO COMFORTABLE

I withhold quite a bit of myself. I have a lot of potential that goes untapped. Though sometimes I perform really well, I rarely come close to my personal best.

NOT COMFORTABLE

I feel alienated here. Much of my energy goes into protecting or hiding myself. I rarely perform well and am very far from reaching my personal best.

In many organizations, leaders try to guess the needs of different groups, such as African-Americans, women, or people over 55. They glean information from the media, a few of the louder or more aggressive constituents, and their own assumptions to create an often inaccurate perception of how other people might feel and what they might need. Some leaders may assume that every Hispanic person favors affirmative action or that every Caucasian person is opposed to it. By taking all responsibility for addressing diversity issues upon themselves, these well-intentioned leaders have taken the power of diversity out of the hands of the people who could most benefit from it. The approach described here minimizes that unintentional depersonalization of diversity by beginning with the person.

USING THE COMFORT ZONES MODEL: PART I
THE PERSONAL ASPECT

1. Assess personal comfort.
2. Identify key comfort factors.
3. Develop personal action plans.
4. Share the lessons.

1. ASSESS PERSONAL COMFORT.

The Comfort Zones Model first invites people to assess how comfortable they feel participating fully in the organization. It's a highly subjective process because comfort is so individualized. All that matters is that people be honest with themselves. There should be no pressure to grade or report their assessment to others.

2. IDENTIFY KEY COMFORT FACTORS.

Next, people identify the key comfort factors that contribute and detract from their ability to participate fully. No one else analyzes them or tells them what they need. Positive factors could include a supportive colleague, a fun environment, or a challenging boss. Negative factors could include anything from a controlling leader to poor self-image, from weak communication skills to feeling disrespected by colleagues.

3. DEVELOP PERSONAL ACTION PLANS.

Once people have identified the key comfort factors, they can develop personal action plans for dealing with the negative ones. They should focus on actions that they could do to address their own situation. It would be completely counter-productive for a person to come away with a list of demands of things that the leader should do without the person having to take any constructive steps. Organizations cannot bend and twist themselves to accommodate every person's needs, fears, and insecurities. For people and organizations to help each other perform, individuals have to be willing to change and grow their skills and confidence.

4. SHARE THE LESSONS.

Depending on the level of trust people feel with each other, they can share their self-analysis in pairs or small groups. By talking and listening to each other, they have a chance to connect at a more personal level than they otherwise might. Placing people in diverse groups that draw upon different cliques or divisions can deeply enrich people's experience, and help build bridges of understanding that may not otherwise exist in the group. Nonetheless, let sharing be a voluntary process in which people disclose only what they want, for, just as this exercise can build relationships, it also can undermine them if people are compelled to reveal more about themselves than they want to.

Once people have examined their personal issues relative to participating fully in the life of the organization, they are in a better position to step back and look at the organization as a whole. For this process, empathy is necessary, and through this process, they will be challenged to develop even more of it. As the exercise shifts from personal to organizational, leaders challenge people to assess how different groups might feel in the organization and what factors might contribute or detract from their performance.

THE COMFORT ZONES MODEL: PART II
THE ORGANIZATIONAL ASPECT

1. Choose groups.
2. Guess personal comfort levels.
3. Identify key comfort factors.
4. Develop personal action plans.
5. Share the lessons.

---

1. CHOOSE GROUPS.

The exercise facilitators choose to consider groups that seem least likely to do well in the organization. For example, a company that cannot retain female engineers might consider one of their groups "women" or even "female engineers." Another organization may find that college graduates do not perform as well as those without a degree and so could consider them a category. One company could have difficulty recruiting international workers and want to better understand why. However the organization chooses the groups for this exercise, it is important to keep them to a manageable number (3-5 groups) at any one time. Otherwise, people can get bored, and the conversations can lose their meaning. Besides, going through the exercise for a few groups generally underscores lessons applicable to all groups.

2. GUESS PERSONAL COMFORT LEVELS.

People step outside themselves to empathize with someone from one of the chosen groups. They try to imagine how comfortable people from this group might feel in the organization. Obviously, participants have to generalize to complete this step. Not all female engineers are going to feel the exact same. Nonetheless, general trends can be used to provide a guess, and that guess can prove useful in the following steps. Leaders may want to remind people that they are generalizing and should not let the exercise interfere with their awareness that individuals from common groups are unique.

3. IDENTIFY KEY COMFORT FACTORS.

Next, people identify the key comfort factors that might contribute to and detract from a group's ability to participate fully. Examining both the positive and negative factors can help people identify what the organization should be doing more of so that they can help everybody become more comfortable.

4. DEVELOP PERSONAL ACTION PLANS.

These plans are different from the plans mentioned in Part I of the Comfort Zones exercise. Those plans addressed actions that people intend to take to help themselves participate more fully in the organization. These plans, however, ask people to step outside themselves by focusing on what they can do personally to make the organization a more comfortable place for others. Rather than delegating all responsibility for creating a constructive environment to their leaders, people accept responsibility for their part in enabling others to participate as fully as possible. One person might commit to stop telling homophobic jokes, whereas another may offer to be a mentor to a person whose learning style needs special accommodations.

5. SHARE THE LESSONS

Leaders should encourage people to share their observations of organizational issues and their plans for addressing them. Getting their ideas out on the table can help them generate plans that build on and support each other. Also, sharing the plans can contribute some informal accountability. If someone commits in her plan to being more supportive of new members of the organization, then others can remind her of her intention if and when she forgets. Still, people should be able to share voluntarily, since some of them will likely devise action plan items that are highly personal.

Indeed, the whole process of discussing diversity can be highly personal for many people, which is part of why such activities can be difficult. Whatever magic leaders hope to create can be dissipated quickly by animosity stirred up uncontrollably in a conversation about diversity issues. Setting some clear guidelines when conducting workshops or guiding conversations can be helpful. Here are some suggestions:

DIVERSITY EXERCISE GUIDELINES

- ➢ Respect confidentiality.
- ➢ Use "I"-statements, not "You"-statements.
- ➢ Listen actively.
- ➢ Refrain from judging other people's perceptions.
- ➢ Go into the process with good intentions.
- ➢ Don't over-emphasize political correctness.
- ➢ Treat people as individuals, not as groups.

The Comfort Zones Model can be a valuable tool for leaders who want the organization and people to work together to bring out the best in everyone. The corollary to the Comfort Zones philosophy is:

COMFORT ZONES COROLLARY

People who feel valued are better able to value others.

As people are respected for what they bring to the organization, they can better respect their colleagues, thus creating a powerful synergy that resonates throughout the organization.

Just as there is no process that responds to the needs of every individual, no single approach to diversity will work for every organization. Leadership magic relies on leaders helping to create the conditions for people to challenge and support each other's pursuit of their best possible performance. By approaching differences from this personal perspective, leaders enable people to leverage the benefits of diversity while minimizing much of the animosity that can be caused by our inherent variety. Diversity doesn't have to be painful. It can be one of an organization's greatest assets.

LEVERAGE DIVERSITY

EXECUTIVE SUMMARY

THE REAL VOYAGE OF DISCOVERY CONSISTS
NOT IN SEEKING NEW LANDSCAPES,
BUT IN HAVING NEW EYES.

MARCEL PROUST

Leadership magic demands a definition of diversity that transcends many contemporary interpretations. Diversity should not be limited to quota counting, regulation following, or politically correcting each other. Organizations that leverage diversity value the inherent uniqueness of every human being, and by acting on their values, can reap the vast rewards of having full participation from their members.

Diversity is most powerful when kept personal. To be creators of magic, leaders note each person's gifts and how they can benefit the organization. Rather than trying to connect with everyone using the same generalized strategies, the leader communicates through many modalities. When diversity is kept personal, much of the animosity that some organizations experience when broaching these subjects is minimized. When people are challenged to come from their personal experience, their comments and actions often carry more heart and less objectification of others.

Organizations create a comfortable environment not just because they want people to feel good, but also because they recognize that when people are comfortable, they participate more fully and therefore learn and continually improve their performance. The direct relationship between comfort and performance makes leveraging diversity a necessity, not a luxury.

Leaders can use the Comfort Zones Model to help people assess their comfort levels in the organization. People could deem themselves "Very," "Mostly," "Not-so," or "Not comfortable" in the organizational context. In this model, individuals rate themselves and thus keep diversity personal.

As people analyze the positive and negative factors that impact their comfort levels, they can develop action plans that will enable them to participate more fully.

Once people have analyzed themselves, they can follow a similar process for the organization as a whole, particularly as it supports groups that tend not to perform as well or feel as comfortable participating fully. At this point, the exercise calls upon people's ability to empathize, an important skill discussed in the chapter about building relationships. Again, individuals create a personal action plan that indicates what each of them can do to help make the organization a more comfortable and productive place.

Creating leadership magic is never about leaders doing the work for others. Leveraging diversity and the other leadership skills examined here demand that people step up and practice these skills themselves. Leaders are guides to personal power, not substitutes for it.

Diversity is one of those areas in which many people feel like victims. It's one of the few topics that can actually cause every person in the room to feel victimized by someone else. By maintaining a personal focus and linking comfort first to participation and then to performance, leaders help people become more proactive and better able to meet their own needs. As they feel valued, they are better able to value others. Diversity becomes a catalyst for the entire organization.

FUNCTIONS
- Redefine diversity.
- Keep diversity personal.
- Assess Comfort Zones.

BENEFITS
- Improved participation
- More learning
- Continuous improvement
- Better performance
- Less animosity
- Greater understanding
- More effective collaboration
- Stronger relationships

LEVERAGE DIVERSITY

SELF-REFLECTION SURVEY

Circle where you are on the scale. Place a star where you would like to be.

		Never				Always
1.	I treat diversity as more than a political issue.	1	2	3	4	5
2.	I respect the unique gifts of each person.	1	2	3	4	5
3.	I value the gifts of my own diversity.	1	2	3	4	5
4.	I participate fully my organization's life.	1	2	3	4	5
5.	I am comfortable in my organization.	1	2	3	4	5
6.	I create a comfortable environment for others.	1	2	3	4	5

OPEN QUESTIONS

Consider, discuss, or write about your thoughts and feelings.

1. My most important qualities are…

2. The ways that I hold back from participating fully in my organization are…

3. The elements that contribute to my full participation are…

4. To make my organization a more comfortable place, I…

III PROCESS

COACH COMMUNICATION
NEGOTIATE CONFLICT

IN TIMES LIKE THESE, MEN SHOULD UTTER NOTHING FOR
WHICH THEY WOULD NOT BE WILLINGLY RESPONSIBLE
THROUGH TIME AND ETERNITY.

ABRAHAM LINCOLN

The ship found itself in the midst of a storm, and here the leader's hard work made the difference between success and tragedy. The crew members couldn't speak much because of the blasting wind and ripping rain, so they made each word count. When hauling a rope or adjusting a sail, they could neither afford to misunderstand each other nor keep repeating their commands. Each crew member listened intently for the words and responses of others; every communication was vital to the success of the ship.

Occasionally, in the heat of the storm, crew members argued about the best strategy. Those who had weathered such storms in the past expressed conflicting ideas about how to best respond to this one. The novices to these conditions held their own untested ideas, some of which might have value. The captain could not afford to let their disagreements literally sink the ship, yet neither could she miss out on the potentially critical recommendations being made. Rather than silencing their arguments, the captain guided them, ensuring that their conflicting opinions were considered appropriately and discussed as thoroughly as possible before she made decisions.

As the ship fought its way through the storm, the captain noticed another craft foundering in the distance. The faces of its crew members were sullen; they seemed overwhelmed and desperate in the perceived impossibility of reaching their destination. Every now and then, the struggling crew members would bark at each other, though the angry commands had little impact since no one listened to anyone else. The storm had pushed them past their limits. While they argued about whether or not to lower a sail, the wind ripped it down for them; while they fought over who should take the helm, a crushing wave disabled the rudder. In the midst of the chaos, it was impossible to identify the captain, if there was one at all.

Organizations depend upon effective processes to make their product, provide their service, and guide their members. Leaders create magic when they attend to the processes through which people communicate with each other and negotiate conflict. The success of nearly every human interaction depends on these two processes, whether the seas be calm, stormy, or uncertain.

COACH COMMUNICATION

Prepare people for success in their communication strategies.

VALUE COMMUNICATION
REVEAL THE MYSTERIES OF ORGANIZATIONAL
   CULTURE
COACH LISTENING SKILLS
COACH SPEAKING SKILLS

VALUE COMMUNICATION

PRECISION OF COMMUNICATION IS IMPORTANT,
MORE IMPORTANT THAN EVER, IN OUR ERA OF HAIR-TRIGGER
BALANCES, WHEN A FALSE OR MISUNDERSTOOD WORD
MAY CREATE AS MUCH DISASTER
AS A SUDDEN THOUGHTLESS ACT.

JAMES THURBER

Through communication, we can strengthen or destroy relationships, and, through relationships, we can strengthen or destroy organizations. There's no way around it. If people cannot effectively exchange ideas, opinions, perceptions, and feelings, they cannot provide the kind of clarity and seamlessness that distinguishes exemplary performance. Communication skills are vital for everyone who ever interacts with someone else, not just salespeople, managers, or human resources personnel.

The chapter on building relationships discusses how any two persons create a relationship, no matter how little they interact in the organization. The CEO who consistently walks by the maintenance worker without saying a word has said an awful lot, or at least left the message open for interpretation and misinterpretation by others. Communication transmits much of the energy exchanged between people and plays a significant role in defining the health of the relationship. Poor communication leads to poor relationships, while consistently open and constructive communication fosters strong ones.

COMMUNICATION IN RELATIONSHIP

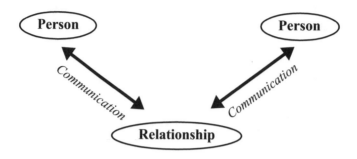

Those who care about their relationships continuously improve their communication skills. Leaders who care about the relationships in their organization—and that would include all leaders who intend to make their organizations the best possible—take on the role of communication coaches. These leaders believe that communication skills can improve, that people can learn to speak and listen more effectively if they are willing to practice.

As personal communication trainers, leaders help people develop the skills that they want to improve and point out areas where they need to work harder. They also recognize that communication styles are closely linked to people's personalities and how they interact with the world. People have distinct communication styles, and the leader who denies this or tries to create a homogenous approach to communication will be sorely disappointed. Nonetheless, leaders would be negligent to pretend that all styles are equally effective.

Too often, less effective leaders let poor communication skills go unchecked in themselves and others, assuming that they can't help someone learn how to communicate, or that communication is a personal matter and should be left alone. If a person's communication skills are terrible, these leaders put a note in their personnel file, ignore them in meetings, or just get rid of them. What a waste. With a little constructive feedback and opportunity to practice, people who want to improve their communication skills can do so, and the whole organization stands to benefit.

The following pages emphasize a few of the most essential elements of communication. To create magic, leaders would not stop with these concepts; but they serve as an excellent place to start. For example, if someone doesn't know the communication codes of the specific culture, it doesn't matter how much she has to say. If someone else hasn't learned to listen, then he can hardly respond well in meetings or even when reading reports. And if people can't speak clearly and confidently, then all of the technological innovations meant to ease communication are only promoting poorly articulated comments in greater number and at greater speed. As an organization improves the essentials of communication, everything else flows much more smoothly.

REVEAL THE MYSTERIES OF ORGANIZATIONAL CULTURE

CULTURE IS A POWERFUL INFLUENCE ON BEHAVIOR
BECAUSE IT IS SHARED WIDELY AND BECAUSE IT OPERATES
WITHOUT BEING TALKED ABOUT, INDEED,
OFTEN WITHOUT BEING THOUGHT OF.

JAMES EVANS AND WILLIAM LINDSAY

Each organization follows its own way of doing things. In every organizational culture, explicit processes and procedures are described in the training manual, handbook, organizational chart, or verbal messages. These are the ways things are supposed to get done. They vary in scope and depth from the operations manual that must be rigidly followed to the guidelines that are more informally presented and followed.

Even more important are those hidden ways of getting things done, the processes through which people really communicate their ideas, secure support, and make things happen. Every culture has them. These are the informal structures through which people operate on a daily basis. In some organizations, meeting agendas are rigorous, and people come prepared to work. In other organizations, such meetings are mostly symbolic because the real work has already been done behind the scenes. In the latter case, the meeting serves as an opportunity to officially accept decisions that already have been made by the influential players.

Understanding these often hidden communication strategies can provide power and direction. Unfortunately, the processes are usually hard to figure out. A person's first year in a new organization can be analogous to sailing on a new ship in a fog. People send all of these confusing signals back and forth between each other. Decisions are made and plans implemented seemingly out of nowhere. It's difficult to figure out whom to believe and to whom—if anyone—one should direct questions and suggestions. A person can consume tremendous energy figuring out who has the power to get things done, what someone's title really means, and what the general expectations are. The hidden guidelines for an organization might even confuse or mislead those who have been in organizations for a long time. Getting promoted can force people to face a whole new set of cultural assumptions that need to be decoded.

Whether people are new or experienced, leaders can save a lot of time and energy by simply teaching how things work in the organization—how they *really* work. Doing so enables people to focus their efforts on taking appropriate action, making more informed decisions, and meeting the expectations by which they are actually being measured. It sets them up for success. They make fewer unnecessary mistakes and are better able to deal with those that inevitably happen.

To clarify the mysteries of the organization's culture for everyone, not just the new members, leaders should have people address the following Questions for Revealing The Mystery Of How Things (Really) Work. Collectively, their answers will reveal a lot about the organizational culture and different perspectives of how it works. Leaders can use this feedback to address areas where conflicting perceptions might be creating inefficiencies. For example, if people respond "no one" to a question about to whom they should take suggestions, the leader has learned something valuable about her organization's effectiveness, particularly if the leader thought that the correct answer was "The Vice President of Operations."

While these questions can be useful tools for discussion, people may answer them more honestly if they can respond anonymously in writing. Remember that the primary goal of leadership magic is to improve the performance of both people and the organization. The process of understanding how the culture really operates meets this goal best when people can be honest without fear of retribution. If people do not think that their supervisor really has decision-making power, or if they don't understand their responsibilities, the leaders of the organization need to know this information promptly so that they can respond appropriately. Leaders should approach this process so that people feel safe to communicate what they really observe.

QUESTIONS FOR REVEALING THE MYSTERY OF HOW THINGS (REALLY) WORK

EXPECTATIONS
Which criteria determine excellent performance for group members? For group leaders?
Who sets and monitors these criteria?
How do I find out if I'm meeting expectations?

DECISION-MAKING
How should I best communicate my input on a decision?
How does my input influence the final decision?
Who makes the final call on important issues?

CONTINUOUS IMPROVEMENT
How should I communicate about a problem I have identified?
How should I make a recommendation?
How good are we really trying to be?

RESPONSIBILITY
How do I know what I am supposed to do?
What can I do when I have made a mistake?
How do I ask for help?

Though these questions are operational, they also are inextricably bound up in communication. To communicate effectively, people need to know the audience they are targeting, the criteria on which their ideas will be evaluated, and the best channel for sending the message. Once they know

these things, they can better assess and develop their skills as communica-
tors. Answering these questions also helps leaders set communication expectations so that they can give people feedback when they are not articu-
lating their ideas well or are failing to hear their colleagues.

Effective communication is the fairy dust of organizational magic.
Without it, the best intentions go nowhere. With it, organizations and people
can be transformed.

COACH LISTENING SKILLS

IF YOU'RE NOT LISTENING, YOU'RE NOT LEARNING.

LYNDON BAINES JOHNSON

Once they have revealed the cultural processes, good leaders coach a
vital communication skill: listening. Organizations need people to listen to
leaders, listen to each other, listen to customers, and listen to the community. Leaders need to listen to everyone. The more actively they can listen,
the more they can absorb potentially valuable information.

Too many people think of listening as a passive skill. They just sit
there and let the words come at them. In the passive mode, they don't
really do anything, except politely nod and smile occasionally. Many leaders make this mistake as well, thinking since leaders are supposed to be
active, they should do something that looks more active, like speak all of
the time. These leaders are so busy offering feedback, running meetings,
and giving orders that they don't hear the potentially valuable messages
constantly coming their way.

Actually, good listeners are very active. They engage their minds and
bodies to take in information. They listen to words, intonations, silences,
and body language to glean not only what is being said explicitly, but also
what important messages lie hidden between the lines. While speaking is a
discrete activity that people can turn on and off, listening is a constant

process. One does not stop listening in order to start speaking, for, even while people speak, they can be listening to the reactions of their audience, checking for understanding, disagreement, or detachment.

While many schools and some organizations offer workshops in public speaking, few if any provide comparable ones for effective listening. To communicate the value they place on listening, leaders should role model it and explicitly inform people that they are listening. Because many people are not accustomed to leaders who actively listen, some of them mistake silent observation for detachment and may need leaders to tell them that their silence springs from respect and helps them pay attention.

Listening requires discipline, and, like any discipline, it requires constant practice. To listen well, leaders need to let go of the notion that they are contributing value only when they are speaking, for this assumption mistakes words for strength and undermines the power of silent attention. The following activities can help leaders listen and can serve as tools to help people listen to each other.

FOUR MAGICAL LISTENING STRATEGIES

1. Silence internal voices.
2. Send listening signals.
3. Reflectively listen.
4. Create a listening filter.

---

1. SILENCE INTERNAL VOICES.

People can't listen to others when their heads are clouded with warnings, recommendations, and other distractions from their own thoughts. Instead of listening to others, some people busily formulate responses to them, just waiting for the other person to pause or take a breath so that they can insert their thoughts. Other poor listeners create "me too" stories when someone else describes a problem he or she faces. Instead of really hearing the other person, the listener tries to think of a similar—or worse—situation. Other internal voices to silence include those that claim that others are stupid or have nothing good to say before they have even begun to speak. Good listeners silence these internal voices as much as possible.

TOOLS FOR SILENCING INTERNAL VOICES

1. Breathe deeply to calm yourself. Anxiety invites voices to create more anxiety.
2. Say to yourself "next" or "no" when a distracting voice speaks. Let the voice go.
3. Open your heart to the other person to reduce distracting judgments.

---

2. SEND LISTENING SIGNALS.

Some speakers need affirmation that they are being listened to, particularly when addressing a leader. Remember that leaders carry more real and perceived power than most people in the organization do. Many people look closely to sense whether or not the leader is validating their opinions or even hearing their input. Use simple signals that can let speakers know that they are being heard, whether or not the listener actually agrees with them. Then, teach these signals to others. These tools are only effective when they are used with sincerity. Pretending to listen rarely works for long.

LISTENING SIGNALS

Verbal Signals	Physical Signals
"I hear you."	Look at person
"I understand."	Face the other person
"Hmm."	Stop doing other work
"Tell me more."	Uncross arms
"Thank you for telling me that."	Find a less distracting place to talk
"Can you please repeat that?"	Turn off phone, pager, TV, computer, etc.

3. REFLECTIVELY LISTEN

Playing the game of "telephone" revealed the difficulty of communication to millions of children. One person started a message, it went around the circle, and, by the time it reached the end, it had become something entirely different, for both intentional and accidental reasons. Unfortunately, after playing the game, few of us were taught how to listen or speak with any more clarity. Reflective listening could very well put the telephone game out of business. It is a simple process that helps both speakers and listeners understand what was said as well as what was meant. Many unnecessary conflicts stemming from miscommunication can be prevented by doing the following.

REFLECTIVE LISTENING PROCESS

1. Listen.
2. Reflect.
3. Check.
4. Clarify.
5. Understand.

---

1. LISTEN.
Let the speaker make a point that is short enough or simple enough for the listener to remember.

2. REFLECT.
The listener says, "What I heard you say was…," then repeats what he or she heard the person say.

3. CHECK.
After repeating it, the listener asks the speaker, "Is that correct?"

4. CLARIFY.

The speaker has many options. He or she can say:

- "Yes" and continue on to the next point; or
- "Yes, but that's not what I meant" and then restate the idea so that it reflects more accurately the speaker's meaning; or
- "No. What I said is…," and repeat the message or restate it in different words or tone to make it clearer to the listener.

5. UNDERSTAND.

The conversation should continue until both parties reach a common understanding of what was meant, even if they do not agree on the statement itself.

The following dialogue between Julia and Randy demonstrates how reflective listening can prevent many simple miscommunications from escalating into a serious problem.

REFLECTIVE LISTENING DIALOGUE EXAMPLE

Randy: I want you to write up this proposal by tomorrow.

Julia: What I heard you say is that this proposal is due tomorrow. Is that correct?

Randy: Not quite. I want you to write it by tomorrow, then put it on my desk so that I can review it before we submit it next week.

Julia: So what I'm hearing you say is that you just want a rough draft. Is that correct?

Randy: No, I want the real thing. Write it for submission. I just want to check it over before we send it in.

Julia: And you want it by the end of the day tomorrow, right?

Randy: Oh no. I need it in the morning.

Julia: *So what I heard is that you want a formal proposal*
         submission on your desk tomorrow morning. You'll
         review it, and then we'll submit it next week.
Randy: Right!
Julia: *Okay, I understand what you want. Now let's talk*
         about how realistic that plan is.

This reflective listening process is particularly helpful when discussing intense or contentious issues because it forces people to slow down and more effectively keep their emotions in check. Instead of panicking when learning that the proposal is due tomorrow morning, Julia first clarifies the expectations. Knowing them, she and Randy can more productively discuss how realistic they are. There is a greater likelihood that both of them will operate with similar expectations.

While the process may seem cumbersome at first, people can use it effectively as they practice. The time invested on the front end making sure both parties share a common understanding eventually saves much time down the road that would otherwise be spent untangling miscommunications.

4. CREATE A LISTENING FILTER

Leaders don't have a lot of time to waste. If they made time to listen to every comment from every person in the organization, they would never be able to do anything else. To protect their time and energy, leaders can create a listening filter to help them maximize the value of the information they take in. As leaders teach other people how to use filters, meetings and conversations can become much more effective.

Leaders create a filter that asks the simple question, "Can I listen to this information now?" The responses help the leader decide whether to actively listen or direct the speaker elsewhere.

THE LISTENING FILTER

```
 _____
(         Can I listen to this information now?        )
 ‾‾‾‾‾‾‾‾‾‾‾‾‾‾‾‾‾‾‾‾‾‾‾‾‾‾‾‾‾‾‾‾‾‾‾‾‾‾‾‾
```

Reasons I Can Listen	Reasons I Cannot Listen
This information is relevant to me.	This information should go to someone else.
I can listen well now.	I am too distracted to listen well.
This speaker often shares valuable information.	This speaker is poorly prepared.
This information solves a current problem.	This information is gratuitous.
This issue is one of my highest priorities.	I am addressing a more urgent issue now.
This information prevents a serious future problem.	This information has no long-term implication.
These ideas need clarification.	We are beating a dead horse.

The listening filter helps leaders listen more effectively, while also helping other people make the most of their time and energy. When using the filter, if the "No" answer comes up, listeners tactfully indicate to the speaker why they cannot listen. They may ask the speaker to find a more appropriate person to tell, to prepare more thoroughly, to come back in two hours, or to simply drop the subject. Leaders should not let listening become a burden. When used well, it should be a tool to increase—not decrease—efficiency.

COACH SPEAKING SKILLS

THE RIGHT WORD MAY BE EFFECTIVE,
BUT NO WORD WAS EVER AS EFFECTIVE
AS A RIGHTLY TIMED PAUSE.

MARK TWAIN

Through speech, people can alienate an entire organization or help it rise to phenomenal heights. They can make themselves appear stupid or convince others of their brilliance. Most importantly, through speech, people provide others access to their minds, intuition, and feelings, and it is this access that leaders can cultivate to create organizational magic. When people speak with clarity, their ideas are transmitted cleanly to others. When they speak with passion, they reveal their intentions and the level of their investment. When they speak with carefully chosen words, they indicate their attention to detail and their desire for comprehension.

To contribute fully to the success of the organization, people need to be willing and able to speak comfortably in pairs and small groups, as well as before large audiences. Anything less impairs a person's ability to participate fully. If a person cannot speak with a handful of others, then his or her teams are always handicapped by his presence. Sure, he might have other valuable traits and thus provide a net gain for his team and organization, but his other talents hardly compensate for the ideas and observations he keeps to himself. He might be the only one with the solution to a major problem! If he is unwilling or unable to share it, then everyone suffers. Even though a person might never be invited to speak before 100 colleagues, leaders would not want the person to withhold an excellent idea because he or she was scared into silence in front of so many peers.

Leaders are in an excellent position to help people develop their speaking skills. Much of the coaching can be informal, such as helping them practice big presentations or giving them feedback after a meeting. Each organization and leader sets different expectations for how people give presentations or speak with each other. Rather than creating some artificially universal structure for speaking, the following list offers some common characteristics of effective speakers.

EFFECTIVE SPEAKER QUALITIES

➤ Good speakers trust themselves.
➤ Good speakers speak with care.
➤ Good speakers set their pace strategically.
➤ Good speakers solicit feedback.

GOOD SPEAKERS TRUST THEMSELVES.

People who do not believe that they have valuable things to say find it hard to persuade others to listen to them. Every member of the organization has valuable perspectives to offer. All of the time? No. There are plenty of times when a person speaks up and the point doesn't go where he intended or fails to persuade others. Such occasional failure comes with any action. Baseball players don't stop going up to bat just because they miss the ball once in awhile. In truth, most people most of the time have valuable comments to offer. A courageous leader will let those who speak too much know that they should cut back. For the vast majority of people, however, speaking up can be an excellent way to develop more trust in themselves, which in turn makes it easier to speak up, which leads to sharing valuable ideas and perspectives.

GOOD SPEAKERS SPEAK WITH CARE.

Oliver Wendell Holmes, Sr. once wrote, "Speak clearly, if you speak at all / Carve every word before you let it fall." Effective speakers capture people's attention in part because they do not waste other people's time with their words. When they have something valuable to say, they say it with confidence and clarity, not necessarily with fancy words. When they do not have valuable words to contribute, they hold their tongue. In particular, they avoid repeating points that others have already made just to get attention or show that they, too, are intelligent. When speaking in professional arenas, they eliminate filler words such as "like," "you know," and "um." A pause makes for better filler than these empty words because it builds suspense for the listener and gives the impression that speakers are choosing their words carefully.

GOOD SPEAKERS SET THEIR PACE STRATEGICALLY.

Sometimes, a speaker has 30 seconds to make a point, at other times, 10 minutes. A good speaker considers how much time she has been given, what she really needs to say, and determines how much time she really needs. Stretching five minutes of good material into a weak ten-minute presentation only makes the speaker and her message look bad. Some audiences want a person to move along quickly; others value a careful cadence. The presentation of words can be at least as important as the content, and good speakers approach both components with the same care.

GOOD SPEAKERS SOLICIT FEEDBACK.

It's difficult to measure the success of communication. Good speakers keep improving their skills by asking listeners for feedback about what they heard and the impressions they have taken away. Speakers then compare those take-aways to their speaking goals. The speaker can also ask about volume, time, body language, eye contact, tone, or any other relevant category.

In most organizations, if two computers were having difficulty exchanging messages, a technician would be brought in right away to address the concern before valuable time or information was lost. If the entire computer network crashed, most leaders would be quick to respond. There is absolutely no reason whatsoever to respond with any less urgency when the communication blocks happen between people. If one person sends a message that does not get to others clearly and accurately, then the leader has a responsibility to address the situation. As a coach, the leader can help the person hone his speaking skills so that the value of his ideas comes through.

Just as some athletic coaches consider the best offense to be a good defense, the best way to become a better speaker is to become a better listener. When people know that they can speak before their colleagues without fear of being cut off, interrupted, or prejudged, they can speak more confidently. When people know that others are really listening to them, they can speak with greater care and less anxiety.

COACH COMMUNICATION

EXECUTIVE SUMMARY

THOUGHTS LEAD TO WORDS;
WORDS LEAD TO ACTION.

MAHATMA GANDHI

Communication lets people share their gifts with the organization. Helping people communicate more effectively enables them to perform more effectively, which make the organization more potent in every arena. By valuing communication, leaders create open channels through which people can transmit ideas, insights, and perspectives. Without such channels, potentially valuable contributions are wasted, never reaching those in the organization who could use them.

Leaders enable people to communicate more effectively by revealing to them the cultural nuances of how things happen in the organization. Rather than forcing people to waste valuable time and energy trying to understand how expectations are communicated, decisions are made, or responsibilities are given, leaders provide them with a road map for how to get things done. The sooner people comprehend how an organization works, the more quickly they can focus on contributing to it. Many communication problems can be prevented if leaders let people know how to get along successfully in the organization.

Before people can become truly proficient in other communication skills, they must possess strong listening skills. There's no way around it. The inability to listen indicates an inability to empathize, or to open one's self to the contributions of others. Leaders can help people improve their listening by teaching them how to silence distracting inner voices, send listening signals, listen reflectively, and create listening filters. These tools take practice.

As people become better listeners, they in turn can become better speakers. Leaders recognize that speaking skills allow people to voice valuable contributions. When these contributions can be expressed with confidence and clarity, the organization blossoms. Good speakers trust themselves, speak with care, strategically set their pace, and solicit feedback.

When people communicate well, organizations make and repeat fewer mistakes, lose fewer ideas, and waste less time and energy. Leaders set the tone for communication. They can demonstrate good skills or model poor ones. They can make it safer for people to speak up or scare them into silence. The most important communication training opportunities happen with every interaction between the leaders and the people they lead. At those moments and through those relationships, people will develop or neglect their communication skills.

FUNCTIONS
- Value communication.
- Reveal the mysteries of organizational culture.
- Coach listening skills.
- Coach speaking skills.

BENEFITS
- Better use of time and energy
- Improved access to ideas
- Fewer mistakes caused by miscommunication
- Better relationships with internal and external constituents
- More clear expectations
- Smoother decision-making
- Organization becomes a more pleasant place to be

COACH COMMUNICATION

SELF-REFLECTION SURVEY

Circle where you are on the scale. Place a star where you would like to be.

		Never			Always
1.	I teach the value of effective communication.	1 2 3 4 5			
2.	I understand our organizational culture.	1 2 3 4 5			
3.	I help others understand our culture.	1 2 3 4 5			
4.	I listen actively to others.	1 2 3 4 5			
5.	I am a thoughtful and effective speaker.	1 2 3 4 5			
6.	I coach better listeners and speakers.	1 2 3 4 5			

OPEN QUESTIONS

Consider, discuss, or write about your thoughts and feelings.

1. I communicate well when…

2. Things that distract me from listening are…

3. The communication skills I would most like to improve are…

4. My plan for improving my communication skills is…

NEGOTIATE CONFLICT

Leverage the power of conflict as a constructive tool for building a better organization.

VALUE CONFLICT
SET CONFLICT GROUND RULES
THE FOUR QUARTER MODEL

VALUE CONFLICT

THE ULTIMATE MEASURE OF A MAN IS NOT WHERE
HE STANDS IN MOMENTS OF COMFORT AND CONVENIENCE,
BUT WHERE HE STANDS AT TIMES OF
CHALLENGE AND CONTROVERSY.

MARTIN LUTHER KING, JR.

Conflict can be an organization's greatest opportunity. Without it, there can be no magic. Magic can only exist when people participate fully in the life of the organization, and rarely can they participate fully without coming into conflict with each other. People bring different experiences and perspectives to the organization, and while the practice of leveraging diversity highlights the value of this variety, it takes the practice of negotiating conflict to really benefit from the myriad ideas and expectations that bring people into conflict with each other. Conflict for the organization is like the fire that transforms wood into heat or water into steam. While it has the potential to destroy, conflict also carries the power to create, and often the skill and intention of the leader tips the scale one way or the other.

In some organizations, leaders avoid conflict, particularly when they see it as a symptom of their inability to control others. Some leaders think that if they were truly effective, everyone would get along all the time, meetings would always proceed smoothly, and no one would ever offend anyone else. To minimize conflict, these leaders may keep meeting agendas free of controversial topics or prevent people from participating in meaningful discussions. The resulting quiet is mistaken for agreement, and the speed with which decisions occur when no one but the leader has input fools some observers into thinking that the organization is efficient.

But dodging or suppressing conflict in the short term only ensures that it will crop up indirectly in the long term, wasting time, energy, and productivity. When the leader forces people to silence their perspectives and feelings to avoid trouble, those thoughts and emotions go underground. People talk about them with their friends and colleagues in the break room, at the bar, or during time that should be dedicated to working together. The organization rapidly becomes a network of suppressed agendas in which tremendous energy is dedicated to figuring out what other people really mean when they say or don't say something.

When they suppress conflict, leaders do not receive the information they need to make the best possible decisions. People learn very quickly to withhold their perceptions for fear of being labeled a troublemaker or disloyal member. They exchange stories about the problems they see and even possible solutions, but all of this discussion happens out of the hearing range of the leaders who don't want to acknowledge that there might be problems.

While some leaders maintain a sense of power by avoiding conflict, others create conflict as the primary means for appearing powerful. They create organizations that pit people against each other so that no one else can develop a power base that might threaten the insecure leader. These leaders want people to argue without resolution, especially about little things that don't really matter. When people don't trust each other and continually block each other's progress, the leader maintains a destructive power over the others. This negative energy cannot be directed to create the best possible organization. The people who rise to the top of such organizations tend to be manipulators who thrive in chaos and use it to their advantage. This situation serves as a sorry compromise for everyone involved because even the leaders who most benefit from this approach to conflict sell themselves short. They settle for mediocrity in themselves and thus bring the organization down with them.

Conflict is too powerful to be misused, and thus the ability to work constructively with conflict becomes one of the most important leadership skills to master. Organizations that can withstand and learn from the conflicts can grow into phenomenal places that truly invite full participation.

Leaders teach people in the organization constructive strategies for approaching conflict first and foremost by being excellent examples. When people see that leaders deal effectively with conflicts between themselves and with other people in the organization, they learn that conflict is not suppressed or abused in the organization. They see that their leaders approach conflict in a mature manner and thus may become more willing to do so themselves.

SET CONFLICT GROUND RULES

CHANGE MEANS MOVEMENT. MOVEMENT MEANS FRICTION. ONLY IN THE FRICTIONLESS VACUUM OF A NONEXISTENT ABSTRACT WORLD CAN MOVEMENT OR CHANGE OCCUR WITHOUT THAT ABRASIVE FRICTION OF CONFLICT.

SAUL ALINSKY

When people join an organization, they learn from leaders about the cultural norms and expectations. They are taught how to convey their ideas and to whom. They learn these standards so that they can add value to the organization. Leaders also ensure that the organization possesses guidelines for negotiating conflict. Sometimes conflicts are strictly personal, other times strictly business, and, often, they fall somewhere in between. Yet common ground rules can be applied to all conflicts within an organization so that people recognize right away how these leaders approach conflict. If the guidelines are not explicitly stated and taught, people will often assume that conflict is handled the same way it is in most organizations: without a clear process, without facilitation, and without an emphasis on being constructive. In short, the random approach most organizations take to conflict is the default mode for most people, unless they are taught to expect and practice something different.

Leaders are responsible for creating a safe space for conflict. Though people need different degrees of safety, in general conflict should be handled in an environment that minimizes interruptions or distractions so that people can truly listen to each other and keep track of their emotions. Some leaders rely on specific processes to indicate that people need to pay more attention or seek privacy because of a conflict. Some also set aside a private and discrete place for negotiating conflict so that a heated discussion between a few people doesn't interrupt or unnecessarily impact others.

With safety and effectiveness as the primary objectives, people can work with leaders to create conflict guidelines which can change with experience as people become more adept at creating conditions for successful conflict negotiation. No matter which formal guidelines the group has accepted, people perceive the real guidelines to be the ones used by the leaders to negotiate their conflicts. In conflict, as in most leadership skills, actions speak far louder than words.

SUGGESTED CONFLICT GROUND RULES

➢ Use "I" statements.
➢ Respect others.
➢ Address the conflict in a timely fashion.
➢ Get outside support.
➢ Breathe and be silent.
➢ Be direct.

USE "I" STATEMENTS.

When people speak about their own experiences and from their personal perspectives, fewer accusations get carelessly tossed about. As well, people are encouraged to accept responsibility for their part in the conflict. The following examples contrast "I" statements with their less productive counterpart, "You" statements.

Example #1

"You" Statement: You make me angry when you do that.
"I" Statement: When you do that, I feel angry.

Note who is in charge of the action in this example. In the first sentence, someone is accusing someone else of making him or her angry, as if the other person controlled the situation. In the second sentence, the person chooses to be angry as a response. By casting feelings as a response for which they assume control and responsibility, people can choose their responses more effectively .

Example #2

"You" Statement: *You should do this, not that.*
"I" Statement: *I think that doing this would be better than doing that.*

The distinction between these two sentences can affect how the listener takes the statement. Many people turn off their listening as soon as they hear, "You should…" They know they're going to hear a sermon, and even if the person means well, the message can get lost. By starting with, "I think that…" the statement is less likely to elicit a defensive response.

RESPECT OTHERS.

It's more difficult to needlessly hurt people whom we respect. By keeping our respect and care for others alive even when we disagree with them, it becomes harder to make sweeping generalizations or hurtful personal attacks that do not add value to the conflict negotiating process. Generally, in a conflict, the people involved have heightened emotions. Without even realizing it, they may be preparing to fight it out or run away from the situation, and so the room for error drops considerably. A single cruel word can escalate the conflict rather than resolve it. Respecting the other person can calm our emotions and help us keep focused on constructively addressing the disagreement at hand. Conflict offers a great time to practice empathizing with others, in part because empathy keeps us calm and open, and in part because empathy may provide keys to understanding other people's perspectives, keys that can unlock conflicts and help us move toward a healthy resolution.

In the last chapter, we discussed a model for relationships that distinguished between people and their relationship. The same model can make conflicts easier to approach constructively. If two people hold opposing views about solving a problem, then the conflict arises between their ideas, not themselves. The differing ideas are not inherently problematic unless people cannot communicate effectively about them. Communication continues to play a significant role in negotiating or escalating the conflict, which is why so many of the guidelines are communication-based.

IDEAS IN CONFLICT

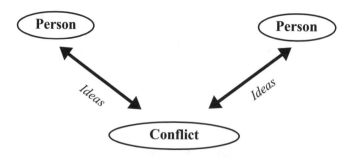

Often, people in such a situation will have common goals and similar commitments to solving the problem. The difference in their ideas stems from having had different experiences and possessing different competencies, not in one person deliberately being stupid or trying to antagonize the other. By seeing the conflict as a separate entity, a leader can encourage them to operate from a common goal of solving the problem. When conflicting parties recognize that they want similar results, they can more easily maintain the respect they have for each other when not in conflict.

ADDRESS THE CONFLICT IN A TIMELY FASHION.

When parties disagree strongly, the feelings can fester beneath the surface for so long that they become rooted in the conflict itself. Festering conflicts cause destructive energies to play out indirectly. Two people trying to work together without addressing a recent conflict are going to have a tough time performing well. They may be worried about the other person's dependability or let their anger escape in petty comments or actions that only exacerbate the situation. Still, some people need time to sort out their thoughts or regain some control over their feelings.

Leaders can encourage people in conflict to let their emotions cool, but not harden. The more quickly people can address a conflict and move on, the more time and energy they can devote to their work together or with others. Buried conflicts can take up a lot of energy. Sometimes, a leader may need to demand that two reluctant people come to the table to address their conflict because it is causing so much turmoil for others in the organization. Other times, leaders may need to separate conflicting individuals until they personally sort out their thoughts and feelings.

GET OUTSIDE SUPPORT.

When people are too close to a conflict, it can be helpful to bring in others who don't have the same personal investment to facilitate the process. When the leader is one of the parties in conflict, an outside person can be particularly helpful because the leader's power and position can make it difficult to address the situation as clearly and constructively as it needs to be addressed. There is no shame in asking for another person to mediate a conflict since that other person can help everyone involved keep the conflict from escalating unnecessarily. By training several people in the organization to handle conflict effectively, leaders maximize the organization's ability to address its conflicts internally.

BREATHE AND BE SILENT.

Two of the best ways to keep cool in the midst of a conflict are to breathe and be silent. Breathing helps people control the tension in their bodies wrought by anger, frustrations, sadness, or fear. As people's muscles tense up, so do their thoughts and their words. The last thing a conflict needs is more tension, so breathing helps keep things calm.

Silence is powerful as well because it gives people time to think and reflect rather than commenting impulsively. When people don't have anything constructive to add, they can be silent and still feel like they are constructively addressing the conflict. Silence is definitely a better option than saying things that are pointless, hurtful, or poorly thought-out. The time between comments also provides an opportunity for ideas and feelings to settle. If the other person said something helpful, then responding immediately may cause the helpfulness to be missed in the flurry of words.

BE DIRECT.

Ultimately, people must resolve their own conflicts. They may go to friends and colleagues for emotional support, yet venting frustrations to those people rarely addresses the conflict constructively. Indeed, facing a conflict by complaining to others or criticizing others behind their backs tends only to exacerbate the situation. Rumors spring up and soon the conflicting parties are hearing reports about themselves, each other, and their situation that are neither accurate nor helpful. Organizations that deal with conflict effectively do their best to directly address the conflict with the people involved. A direct approach keeps conflicts from spiraling out of control.

These suggestions can help organizations begin making their own guidelines. The process of discussing how people hope to benefit from conflict and what they need to help make conflict constructive can make for a fascinating and educational conversation. Leaders who are willing to talk about conflict and to acknowledge that it will happen in their organizations take a significant step toward creating healthy conditions for negotiating conflict.

People will find it refreshing and perhaps a bit scary to work with a leader who really wants to resolve conflicts constructively and who possesses some of the skills or other resources necessary to do so effectively.

It's okay for people to feel nervous when they hear that their leaders intend to negotiate rather than bury or deny conflict. After all, few people have had positive experiences with conflict, particularly in an organizational setting. Even fewer of them feel prepared to handle conflict well themselves, no matter how much they believe in its value. Thus, leaders who intend to negotiate conflict prepare themselves and others to handle it well.

THE FOUR QUARTER MODEL

WITHOUT HONEST CONFLICT,
A GROUP DIES OF A DISEASE WE CALL CONFLUENCE,
WHICH IS EVERYBODY MAKING 'NICE-NICE.'

BILL KAUTH

Most of the time, people can work through conflicts by relying on their instincts, communication skills, and supportive colleagues. Sometimes, however, conflicts become too difficult to handle even when the opposing parties apply common sense and the organization's guidelines. The difficulty may stem from the complexity of the problem or the intensity of the emotions it arouses. When that occurs, a tool such as the Four Quarter Model can clarify the issues. The following model is recommended for a whole organization to adopt because it's fairly easy to learn, easy to remember, and very effective. But it also requires a lot of practice before organizations benefit from its effectiveness.

People should practice the Four Quarter Model with others who are already adept at using it so that they can see how it flows and how good facilitators respond to unexpected situations. I also recommend practicing on relatively minor conflicts before applying this approach to major ones. Though a model such as this can be more effective than having no conflict strategy at all, it can also be unwieldy if people are not accustomed to moderating conflicts.

I include a basic description of the Four Quarter Model because it can help leaders keep conflicts organized in their own heads by sorting out various issues. This sorting process in itself can eliminate much of the anxiety and confusion around a conflict, even if it doesn't lead directly to resolution. By teaching the model to others, leaders can help people with whom they work develop a common approach to conflicts.

These steps follow the order that I have found most effective, though I have witnessed others switch around the first three steps and do very well. I do not recommend skipping any steps altogether, for each one challenges people to consider a valuable aspect of the conflict. The four quarters form a circle that progresses in a clockwise direction from Data to Judgment to Feeling and culminating in the upper left-hand quarter with Want.

FOUR QUARTER MODEL

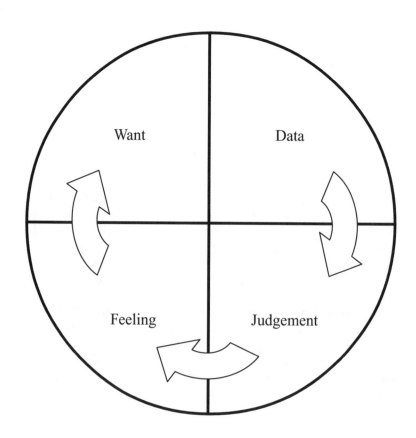

FIRST QUARTER: DATA

Essential Question: What happened?

A person first identifies and states what happened in the conflict. Each person involved in the conflict describes these facts from his or her perspective, but is careful to avoid putting their judgments on things. They are only restating, as clearly and objectively as possible, what they think happened in the conflict .

DATA EXAMPLE #1

Bad data: *You're late because you don't care about us.*
Good data: *You showed up at 9:15. The meeting started at 9:00.*

Note how the first statement adds an assumption about the other person's motivation, while the second one simply restates what happened. The assumption revealed in the first statement indicates a source of anger that probably fuels this conflict, but treating the assumption as if it were a fact is unhelpful since the person doesn't really know why the other one showed up late.

DATA EXAMPLE #2

Bad data: *That's a stupid idea. You obviously weren't thinking.*
Good data: *We need a solution to the problem that we can implement for under $20,000. Your proposal would cost at least $50,000.*

If a supervisor were giving someone the feedback statements listed above, he or she would meet with far more success using the second statement, in part because it makes fewer assumptions, but also because it provides some direction for the person. The cost needs to come down, or the budget needs to go up. The supervisor can't be sure why the proposed solution is over-budget and so, rather than make assumptions, she sticks to the facts.

It's hard to argue passionately about data, though generally people perceive events differently. Still, laying the facts out early in the process of negotiating conflict can help everyone identify key discrepancies and clarify events without hurling accusations that cause defensiveness or hurt feelings. Most importantly, the exercise of separating data from judgments and feelings compels people in conflict to sort through what really happened. Sometimes in doing so, they recognize that the person with whom they disagreed did not really intend to offend or hurt them, and that their conflict is not a personal attack.

SECOND QUARTER: JUDGMENTS

Essential Question: What judgments do I have about you and me?

The second stage of sorting out a conflict requires stating one's assumptions or perceptions about the conflict. These judgments are usually based on the person's past experience and are filtered through the biased lenses with which each of us views life. Whether or not the judgments are accurate is unimportant at this stage; the key issue is that a person be clear about the difference between what really happened and what personal spin he has put on the event.

In example #1 above, the bad data statement is not good data because it ends with a judgment, *"...because you don't care about us."* Even if this statement is totally false and the other person actually does care about the group, having made this statement reveals an underlying fear that is probably making the conflict worse than it needs to be. What if the person arrived late because of a flat tire or a personal crisis? What if she arrived late because she was lost or trying to perfect her notes for the meeting? The speaker can't even consider these plausible alternatives because he is so fixated on his fear that the other person doesn't care.

When the speaker in the second example says, "That's a stupid idea. You obviously weren't thinking," she has offered two judgments, one about the person and one about her idea. Though some listeners could interpret the comments as cruel, they do serve the purpose of letting the listener know the speaker's point of view. Two issues will need attention. Both parties need to assess the validity of the idea as well as the speaker's perception that the other person wasn't thinking. By distinguishing their judgments from their facts, they can help illuminate the conflict rather than stimulate wasteful debate about each other's intentions.

THIRD QUARTER: FEELINGS

Essential Question: How do I feel about this situation?

Feelings can drive conflicts on and on, particularly if a conflict has stirred up anger or pain that no one is willing to let go. Feelings can also add heart to a conflict in a way that facts alone could never do. For example, imagine if someone showed up late to a meeting or didn't follow through on an idea, and his supervisor said, "I'm sad when you aren't there," or "I feel hurt when you don't follow through." Suddenly, the conflict is not about one person's carelessness, but about its personal effect on someone else.

Separating the feelings from the data and judgment also helps the speaker focus on what is going on internally. Simply saying "I'm angry" can help release some of the anger. Instead of suppressing it so that it leaks out in other indirect ways, verbalizing the feeling gives it some air to breathe, a personal acknowledgment, and the opportunity to move on.

Some people aren't used to talking about feelings, and so they confuse feelings and judgments when they say things like, "I feel that you don't care about me." Feelings are emotions, not perceptions. They include emotions such as mad, sad, glad, ashamed, afraid, and excited. While leaders shouldn't be overly rigid about what constitutes a feeling, they can challenge people to better understand their emotions by keeping feelings and judgments separate.

FOURTH QUARTER: WANTS

Essential Question: What do I want out of this situation?

People can spend hours rehashing their data, judgments, and feelings, and yet accomplish little constructive resolution. Often in conflict, all parties feel like victims because they see themselves as misunderstood, unappreciated, undervalued, or otherwise treated less respectfully than they deserve. The victim approach to conflict goes nowhere, because usually everyone involved feels treated as the victim. If everyone is the victim, then who could the perpetrator be? When people get trapped in this victim-oriented cycle, no constructive resolution to the conflict can emerge because no one sees that he or she has the power to take the conflict to a healthier place.

To help people move out of their victim mode, the leader can ask a simple question: What do you want? This question challenges people to consider what they want to get out of the conflict, which puts them back into a position of power. Though they may have felt powerless in their victimhood, stating their wants forces them to think constructively about the situation perhaps for the first time. Occasionally, people will be so consumed by expressing their anger or rehashing the details of their conflict that they can only say, "I don't know," when they are asked what they want. These people need some reflection time before continuing so that they can identify what they want.

Expressing what they want empowers people to move through the conflict more successfully even though the other parties may not be able to give them what they want. By continuing to dialogue with good intentions, people often can reach resolution. See how this can work in the following example:

STATING WANTS EXAMPLE

Angela: *I want you to show up at 9:00 A.M. every morning.*
Clay: *I can't do that. I take my daughter to school at 8:45 A.M. I want you to help me develop a more flexible schedule.*
Angela: *Okay, we can try that, but I want you to follow it closely so that I know when I can count on you to be here.*
Clay: *That's fair. Let's give it a shot.*

At times, even this fourth step of the model is not sufficient to negotiate a conflict successfully. Eventually, however, people can become quite adept at using this model and sometimes can skip right to the fourth step. As they train themselves to better handle conflict, they recognize more clearly what they want and can bypass some of the other steps.

The Four Quarter Model is a powerful tool for raising awareness about conflict and then helping people negotiate it. The following dialogue shows how two people might use the model to address a conflict between them.

USING THE FOUR QUARTER MODEL

Jackie: *I left a file on my desk. When I came back it was gone. You were the only one here in the office. I think you took it and that makes me angry! I want you to give it back. Now!*

Carlos: *Slow down! I can understand your anxiety about the file since you've been working on it all week, but I was not the only one in the office. One of the custodians came through while you were out. Maybe he accidentally took it or threw it away. I think you're jumping to conclusions because you don't trust me, and I'm angry. I want you to trust me and stop accusing me of taking it.*

Jackie: *Did you see which custodian?*

Carlos: *Yes, I did.*

Jackie: *I would appreciate it if you would help me find the custodian. You're right; I jumped to conclusions, and I want to trust you as well. I'm sorry. Could you please help me find it?*

Carlos: *No problem.*

In this exchange, Jackie is clearly upset, and Carlos has enough empathy for her to stay engaged instead of just blowing up at the false accusation. Once she sees her mistake, Jackie has the courage to apologize and

ask for help, two key steps that can quickly cool a conflict before it ex-
plodes. The terms such as "data" and "judgment" are not evident in the
dialogue, though their use is evident as described below.

FOUR QUARTER ANALYSIS

DATA

> Jackie: File on desk; file missing; no one else in office (incorrect).
> Carlos: Custodian in office; Jackie was working on file all week.

JUDGMENTS

> Jackie: I think you took it.
> Carlos: You don't trust me.

Feelings

> Jackie: Anger.
> Carlos: Anger.

WANT

> Jackie: Give it back (impossible); help me find it.
> Carlos: Trust me; stop accusing me.

No single process or training can successfully negotiate every conflict,
nor are there any leaders who can eliminate the distracting and sometimes
painful side-effects of conflict. The Four Quarter Model is just one tool
among many that can help organizations transform conflict from obstruc-
tion into opportunity.

When leaders bring tools for negotiating conflict into their organizations, they build in time for people to practice. By role playing hypothetical conflicts, people can practice identifying and using the Four Quarter
Model without the stress caused by the intensity of a real conflict. They
also evaluate their progress as they practice negotiating conflict. Was the
resolution effective? Did both sides leave satisfied? What else could have
been said or done? Were the guidelines followed? Were they effective?

Above all else, leaders practice what they preach, especially when
working with conflict. They transcend their potentially wounded or fright-

ened egos so that they can approach conflict intelligently and constructively. They manage their own conflicts as directly as possible and in as
timely a manner as possible, for they cannot afford to waste their energy
wallowing in the anxiety of an unresolved conflict.

NEGOTIATE CONFLICT

EXECUTIVE SUMMARY

HE THAT WRESTLES WITH US
STRENGTHENS OUR NERVES, AND SHARPENS OUR SKILL.
OUR ANTAGONIST IS OUR HELPER.

EDMUND BURKE

Conflict has the power to help create a magical organization or to destroy it from within. There is no realistic way to deny or avoid conflict because it is the inevitable result of unique individuals coming together. Conflicts result when people's different ideas, perspectives, and expectations meet in apparent opposition. Suppressing conflict only drives it beneath the surface so that it plays out in dangerous ways for everyone. When handled constructively, conflict provides excellent learning opportunities because ideas are openly discussed, tensions are addressed and resolved, and organizations can shed what doesn't work in exchange for what might work better.

Leaders who appreciate the value of conflict set ground rules to create a safe environment for handling the feelings that can arise when people disagree. Some common ground rules include having people use "I" statements, respecting others, being timely, getting outside support, breathing and being silent, and being direct. While no magic formula exists for making conflicts easy to negotiate, these guidelines help people stay constructive and focused on moving beyond the conflict rather than wallowing in it.

The Four Quarter Model provides a strong tool for negotiating conflicts because it helps conflicting parties organize their reactions and focus on the outcomes. The model makes it more difficult to get stuck in a conflict. Each quarter describes a focus area for the people involved. Each person starts by relating the *data* about what happened or what was said that has led to the conflict. Then, the person describes the *judgments* that he or she has formed about the other person's intentions. These judgments often reveal the assumptions that have exacerbated the conflict. Next, the person tells about the *feelings* that in response to the situation. Simply acknowledging these feelings helps get them under control and lets both parties know what emotions are activated beneath the surface.

Finally, and most importantly, the Four Quarter Model compels the conflicting parties to describe what each of them *wants*. This want statement compels people to abandon a victim orientation by seeing that they have the power to articulate their own needs and desires. Though the other parties may not be able to give them what they want, even figuring out their wants can help people get themselves unstuck.

Most people, including leaders, have not had constructive experiences with conflict. Whatever models or procedures organizations develop to negotiate conflict well, practicing often in hypothetical situations and role-plays will help everyone develop the confidence and ability to deal more effectively with real conflicts. Evaluating their conflict negotiation processes helps organizations continuously improve their approach and gives individuals a sense of how they can become more effective conflict negotiators.

The leaders who can help their organizations leverage the power of conflict open whole new vistas of possibility. They empower people to participate fully in the life of the organization because people no longer have to suppress so many of their thoughts and ideas for fear of getting into disagreements that spiral out of control. With conflict as a tool rather than an obstacle, people can focus their energies and intelligence on performing at their best. The heat of conflict no longer burns so harshly; instead, it makes leadership magic.

FUNCTIONS
- Value conflict.
- Set conflict ground rules.
- Use and teach the Four Quarter Model.

BENEFITS
- More open expression and discussion of ideas
- Better decision-making
- More effective use of time and energy
- Improved relationships
- More active participation
- Less negative tension
- Fewer distractions
- Less sabotage

NEGOTIATE CONFLICT

SELF-REFLECTION SURVEY

Circle where you are on the scale. Place a star where you would like to be.

	Never				Always
1. I teach the value of negotiating conflict.	1	2	3	4	5
2. I deal with conflict constructively.	1	2	3	4	5
3. I use ground rules for dealing with conflict.	1	2	3	4	5
4. I help people address conflict constructively.	1	2	3	4	5
5. I separate perceptions, feelings, and desires.	1	2	3	4	5
6. I practice negotiating conflict.	1	2	3	4	5

OPEN QUESTIONS

Consider, discuss, or write about your thoughts and feelings.

1. When I am in a conflict with someone, I usually...

2. When people around me are in conflict with each other, I usually...

3. My ideal personal approach to conflict would be to...

4. My plan for improving my conflict negotiation skills is...

IV PERFORMANCE

GUIDE RITUALS
TAKE BOLD RISKS

DESTINY IS NOT A MATTER OF CHANCE,
IT IS A MATTER OF CHOICE.
IT IS NOT SOMETHING TO BE WAITED FOR;
IT IS SOMETHING TO BE ACHIEVED.

WILLIAM JENNINGS BRYAN

As every captain knows, a ship cannot afford to depend entirely upon one person, so the wise captain created a ritual that would build bonds between the crew members. At every shift change, the captain pulled together the old and new shifts for a brief meeting. The old shift members told the others about their course and the condition of the boat. Also, they addressed unique challenges caused by unexpected currents or weak winds. As the old shift members passed their responsibilities to the new shift, each said something familiar to inspire the others. The new shift reviewed their assignments and checked to make sure everyone could perform their responsibilities. As the new shift took their positions and the old shift went on break, the captain thanked them all for their hard work. The process lasted no more than five minutes and enabled the ship to move on seamlessly.

One day, the ship came upon an unmapped island. To land and explore it would take them at least two days off course, yet many crew members were fascinated by the possibility of discovering uncharted land. Still others wanted to continue the voyage, uninterrupted. The captain consulted with the crew, reviewed the charts, and checked the winds and currents. Then she stepped out onto the bow of the boat to be alone. The captain deeply felt her responsibility for the safety of ship and crew, as well as her duty as a sailor to venture into the unknown. There was no right answer about whether or not to land, for the data could support either decision. But her intuition made it clear. She knew what she must do.

Organizations and people ultimately are defined by their actions. Words and processes are of little value unless they translate into effective action. Magic emerges from the combined energies of people coming together around the common mission and making it a reality. When people act deliberately and thoughtfully, they can accomplish almost anything.

GUIDE RITUALS

Energize and focus people through meaningful, inspiring activities.

MAKE EVERY GATHERING SPECIAL
HONOR THE MISSION AND VISION
CHECK IN
CHECK OUT
CELEBRATE SUCCESS

MAKE EVERY GATHERING SPECIAL

DON'T MAKE SOMETHING UNLESS
IT IS BOTH NECESSARY AND USEFUL;
BUT IF IT IS BOTH NECESSARY AND USEFUL,
DON'T HESITATE TO MAKE IT BEAUTIFUL.

SHAKER RULE OF THUMB

Every time people come together around a common objective, they can approach it as a special moment worthy of their finest effort or as just another routine task. They can be inspired or jaded, focused or distracted, and guided by the mission or flailing in search of direction. Many groups function somewhere in between, occasionally reaching moments of excellence as well as sinking to discouraging levels of ineffectiveness. One day, the team turns out a stellar performance, and the next they can't even get the crowd—or customers—on their side. This inconsistency wears group members out, frustrating them almost as much as it frustrates the leaders who are held accountable for keeping them motivated and performing well.

Fortunately, performance doesn't have to be so random. Many leaders institute technological control systems to help even out the human variability in their organizations. Others rely on supervisors to ride people as drill sergeants would. Lately, more organizations have taken to trusting people to monitor their own performance. Each of these strategies has its place and can prove helpful. Yet another approach is often overlooked which complements these responses and helps focus the entire organization.

Leaders inspire excellence by guiding rituals that focus people's energy and attention on the purpose and success of the organization. Rituals don't have to be spiritual or hokey; they simply require that people design some special activity around an ordinary event. After all, that's what leaders who guide magical organizations do every day: they create extraordinary results from ordinary resources. These leaders can help transform a team of average players into real contenders who can innovate in a mature industry, generate sustainable financial growth in the midst of economic stagnation, or otherwise exceed expectations.

Just as communication helps people create connections, rituals help people deepen those relationships. Rituals can serve as transformers along an electrical circuit that alter the voltage and current passing along the wire to make them appropriate for the task at hand. If the current is too strong, it can blow the wiring on the other end; if it is too weak, it may not provide the necessary energy; and, if it fluctuates too much, it may not prove useful at all.

Rituals can be found whenever people create meaningful opportunities for connection, reflection, and growth. Well-crafted rituals provide a chance to slow down and concentrate on a delicate task or get energized about a rigorous challenge that demands tremendous effort. The rituals are generally marked by some kind of exercise that complements the primary activity of the organization. For example, if the group has come together for a meeting, anything that they do together to help make that meeting more effective could be considered a ritual. If a team gathers near the sidelines before a big game to motivate each other with a cheer or warm-up drill, and they are excited about it and let themselves get into it, they are using rituals to enhance their performance. On the other hand, a ritual has not happened if the coach half-heartedly calls people together while everyone looks around vaguely and ties their shoes, and the coach and a few players mumble, "Go, team." That mockery of tradition doesn't work because if it does anything, this non-ritual has only exacerbated what promises to be a less than stellar performance.

Powerful rituals are characterized by common characteristics that help leaders and people work together to meet the needs of the group. Leaders would probably choose different rituals with hockey players or construction workers than with youth groups or social workers, yet they may be different only in detail, not in essence. The following list captures vital elements of effective rituals:

VITAL ELEMENTS OF EFFECTIVE RITUALS

- ➤ Be inclusive.
- ➤ Be inspiring.
- ➤ Concentrate.
- ➤ Emphasize purpose.
- ➤ Be relevant.

BE INCLUSIVE.
Design rituals in which everyone can participate comfortably and even eagerly.

BE INSPIRING.
Motivation can appear as a group of cheering people or simply as the gleam in someone's eye.

CONCENTRATE.
Distraction-free rituals compel people to pay attention to the task at hand.

EMPHASIZE PURPOSE.
Rituals remind people why they are gathering right now or working so hard and how this activity bears upon the organization's deeper purpose.

BE RELEVANT.
Each task deserves a ritual that shows its value and meets the needs of the people performing it.

Using rituals with adults can be a scary leap. Many leaders fear that people will be cynical or reluctant to participate in activities that may seem too touchy-feely, though a leader who is sincere and attentive to his or her audience can develop rituals that are non-threatening and appealing to most people. Consider which leaders rely on rituals the most. Athletic coaches and military leaders often use rituals to unify people, particularly when challenges become most intense. For example, a team that has performed the same ritual before every game and practice all season long can use it to calm nerves and concentrate players before the big championship game. A military team whose members review their objectives and responsibilities and make eye contact with each other before going into action is more likely to have each member focused and knowledgeable about his or her role. Religious leaders tap the power of rituals as well, particularly when they are performed sincerely and when people find the rituals relevant and inspiring.

Many people seek meaning and connection through organizations. They want to do more than just go to work, do their jobs, and go home. Parties and other social gatherings will always serve an important role in pulling people together, and giving them a chance to have fun getting to know each other, yet leadership magic takes this concept further because the rituals revolve around more than just social connections. The rituals that inspire greater performance also center on the organization's purpose and processes. They are linked directly to the organization's mission and the context through which people interact.

One way to elicit buy-in from members of the organization is to include them in creating rituals. Leaders don't have to do it all. In fact, many of the best rituals will come from within the organization, leaving the leader to recognize them and promote their consistent adoption. For the most part, they won't be called rituals. People don't usually say, "Hey Joe, I've got this great ritual we can do before we head out to the building site." Maybe some people will choose those words, but most will be more subtle. As long as people recognize that there is value in coming together to motivate and prepare themselves before doing something, they will often devise their own rituals. If calling it a ritual turns people off because it has religious connotations or seems too New Age, then select a different word such as process, activity, or exercise. Don't let the terminology interfere with the value that rituals can provide.

Rituals shouldn't be so formalized that they smother the very spirit that made them effective in the first place. Rituals can emerge spontaneously and then go away once they've served their purpose. Most often, good rituals continue to evolve over time as new leaders and other group members add their own touches. Once a ritual gets inscribed into some formal operations manual, it likely becomes just another habit or process, a burdensome chore that people perform because they are supposed to, not because it contributes any value to the group. Thus, leaders keep guiding new rituals and adapting old ones so that they remain relevant and fresh. They can't just create a ritual once and expect it to grow on its own.

The rest of this chapter describes some of the most important opportunities for rituals. To create magic, leaders help build rituals around these areas, at least. As they prove effective, other rituals will spring up from within the organization in ways and with power that a leader could never have dreamed up alone. Giving people a chance to commit to the organization's mission is an excellent way of bringing them into the organization, and a simple ritual can accelerate how quickly they invest themselves in the group's success. Rituals that mark the beginning and end of an activity help them focus in an often busy world, while those that celebrate success provide incentives that motivate many people at least as well as financial rewards, if not better.

HONOR THE MISSION AND VISION

A VISION WITHOUT A TASK IS BUT A DREAM,
A TASK WITHOUT A VISION IS DRUDGERY,
A VISION AND A TASK
IS THE HOPE OF THE WORLD.

FROM A CHURCH IN SUSSEX, ENGLAND, C. 1730

To motivate others, leaders must believe that their organizations are important, that they provide some service or product to the community that adds value to people's lives. Occasionally, organizations grow so busy and tactically focused that they lose sight of the purpose that supposedly drives them. The big picture fades into obscurity, and the inspiration on which the organization was founded fails to support the people who most need it to guide them. A mission is hardly important if no one actively pursues it.

Rituals that honor the organization's mission and vision keep the purpose in the minds of its people so that they can focus their efforts to make it a reality. It's good to have rituals that ensure every person recognizes and commits to the mission in a significant way when they first join or recommit to the organization. The following two rituals are particularly effective and easy to integrate into the normal operations of most organizations.

HONORING STRATEGY #1: THE PLEDGE

The pledge ritual is just one example of how leaders can promote this buy-in because it compels people to not only hear and understand the mission but also formally commit to supporting its success. That extra step is what helps push people toward higher levels of performance.

The Pledge Ritual

1. Display the mission.
2. Bring the people.
3. Say the mission.
4. Sign it.
5. Display it.
6. Reaffirm it.

1. DISPLAY THE MISSION.

    Find a public space to display the mission. Some might use a wall, others a portable canvas, and still others might display it in cyberspace, depending on the nature of their organization. Place the mission in a central location and make it as physically tangible as possible. The words should be large enough to be seen from a good distance. Leave some space around the mission. Keep reading, and you'll see why.

2. BRING THE PEOPLE.

    Have important members of the organization gather near the mission statement. Even if they have already gone through this process, their presence lends support for those going through it for the first time. Special partners of the organization might be included in this process, though leaders should be careful about including too many outside people lest they diminish the pledge's internal value or offend others within the organization.

3. SAY THE MISSION.

    Have people stand and say the mission aloud. This is not some bizarre cult-like experience, but an exercise to register the mission in the participants brains more completely than if they just read it off a handout. Say it with zest and enthusiasm, in a somber drone, or in whatever tone is appropriate, but do consider the tone. It affects the interpretation of the words.

4. SIGN IT.

    This is where the mission becomes a pledge. Ask people to come forward to sign the wall, canvas, board, or screen on which the mission has been written. Their signature demonstrates a commitment to supporting the mission. It's not a legally binding pledge, but a ritualized one that requires stepping out publicly in support of the organization's mission.

5. DISPLAY IT.

Keep the mission and its accompanying signatures in a centrally visible location. As people look at it on their own time, rediscover their signatures, or show others where they signed on, the mission and its value will be reinforced.

6. REAFFIRM IT.

Every now and then, when a special event occurs or a new group of people needs to sign on, require the group as a whole to repeat the process, though they should only sign it once. Don't do formal exercises with the mission every day or at every meeting, or it can lose its value. Reaffirmation should occur occasionally with sincerity, not out of forced habit.

The pledge ritual affirms people's commitment to the organization by placing the mission at the center. At the same time, it recognizes that the organization is only as effective as the individuals who support it by having their personal signatures surround it. The ritual carries strong symbolic value that can energize people and heighten their awareness of the mission while strengthening their commitment to it.

Some leaders might think that the pledge ritual seems overly formal or solemn for fast-moving organizations or those with transitory members. However, the more fragmented or transitory the organization, the more important the pledge process can be because it provides a common experience around the mission and immediately indicates everyone's value. The more disjointed or resistant the group, the more powerful the pledge can be for encouraging them to literally "sign on" with the organization's mission.

HONORING STRATEGY #2: THE VISION

On a more regular basis, organizations can keep people aware of the mission and vision by weaving them into the fabric of meetings or other activities. By visioning for a few minutes before an event gets underway, the leader reminds people how the event relates to the underlying purpose of the organization. The explicit reminder helps people make decisions and work with the purpose closer to the front of their minds. The process looks like this:

THE VISIONING PROCESS

1. Tell a powerful story.
2. Link the story to the vision.
3. Link the vision to the upcoming activity.

---

1. TELL A POWERFUL STORY.

The leader chooses a true story about the organization's impact on someone whom it is designed to serve. The story should be brief and compelling so that it energizes people. One could also use a quote or fictional story, though these are far less powerful since they don't come from the organization's own experience.

2. LINK THE STORY TO THE VISION.

After the story has been told, connect it to the vision or mission of the organization. Be able to answer "So what? What has this got to do with our purpose?" This is the moral of your story.

3. LINK THE VISION TO THE UPCOMING ACTIVITY.

Once the story has been connected to the vision, bring them both back to the upcoming activity. Be able to answer "So what? What has our purpose got to do with this activity?"

Before an important meeting, a two- or three-minute visioning process can remind people about the relevance of all of the logistical nuts and bolts that they're about to discuss. Before people begin work on the construction site in the morning, the contractor can describe for them the beauty of the end product they are building, point out a particularly elegant piece of craftsmanship, or tell them how it will be used. In any context, visioning enables the leader to honor the organization's purpose.

Though leaders should model the visioning process often, they can stimulate greater interest and awareness by inviting others to lead these sessions. By taking a few minutes to train people to create vision stories and link them to the activity, the leader helps people become even more aware of the links than they might otherwise be. People also improve their own leadership skills by developing their ability to inspire others, so delegating a visioning ritual can be a great way to teach leadership. And as another not-so-minor benefit, people who lead the visioning are more likely to become invested in the activity itself and better able to engage their friends and colleagues.

Often, people complain that their work lacks meaning. Usually, however, the problem lies not in the work itself, but in their ability to see the meaning behind it. Leaders use rituals to connect people with the organization's purpose. Once connected, people are more likely to make better choices and perform with greater enthusiasm. Rituals that honor the mission and vision set the stage for personal and organizational success.

CHECK IN

GENUINE BEGINNINGS BEGIN WITHIN US,
EVEN WHEN THEY ARE BROUGHT TO OUR ATTENTION
BY EXTERNAL OPPORTUNITIES.

WILLIAM BRIDGES

Intention is everything. Assuming that everyone possesses the same skills, the key differentiator between those who rise to great heights and those who wallow in failure becomes how well they *use* their skills. Confidence plays a huge part in this distinction, though as people achieve more and more authentic success, their confidence should increase. In the meantime, leaders can promote success by guiding rituals that prepare people to be their best even before they have begun an activity. People who go into an activity with clear goals and strong, focused energy outperform their less-prepared peers nearly every time.

Too often, leaders begin activities without consciously considering the impact of the message they send on the effectiveness of the group. Opening a meeting with a joke or two can get people laughing, but then what? The laughter has loosened them up, but additional steps can concentrate their now-loose energy. Some leaders don't open with anything. People show up at work, go to their desk or station, and just begin.

While a few people are intrinsically motivated to do well and so inspire themselves, many others benefit from rituals that help them get going. It takes more than a cup of coffee to enable people to reach their highest performance. Most of us need an opportunity to shake off the distractions that we have brought from other parts of our lives to the activity at hand. If a teacher walks into a classroom still thinking about an argument she had with her spouse, she can hardly attend to the students' needs, particularly if she is busy trying to pretend she isn't upset. A fire fighter shaking off a bad dream cannot possibly drive the truck to a fire as safely and efficiently as he would if he were already alert.

Check-in rituals help people more effectively begin a meeting or activity. They enable people to publicly voice their thoughts, feelings, concerns, or plans based on the needs of the moment. Presenting and agreeing to guidelines ahead of time helps ensure that the ritual stays focused and doesn't waste time, energy, or commitment. The following guidelines work well for many groups. Leaders should modify them to fit their needs.

CHECK-IN GUIDELINES

1. One speaker, many listeners.
2. Pass it on.
3. No comment.
4. Keep it personal.
5. Set the time.
6. Everyone participates.

1. ONE SPEAKER, MANY LISTENERS.

Only one person speaks at a time while everyone else actively listens. No one does work during the check-in or carries on side-conversations.

2. PASS IT ON.

Once a person has spoken, he or she signals completion by saying or doing something that the group has agreed upon: i.e. hit a bell, pass a ball, give someone a high-five, say, "I'm in."

3. NO COMMENT.

People do not comment on each other's check-ins and don't discuss them until everyone has checked in, if at all. Sometimes, just letting people say something is enough, and the leader won't want them going on tangents instead of focusing on their responsibilities. Other times, someone may check in with information that the group needs to address later, and the leader may want to plan accordingly.

4. KEEP IT PERSONAL.

People don't check in about someone else in the group. Most of the time, a check-in is not an opportunity for people to say how angry they are at someone else. That issue requires a different process that follows the organization's strategy for negotiating conflict.

5. SET THE TIME.

The check-in should have a time frame. Some check-in rituals may last for a total of one minute, others for 20 minutes, depending on the size of the group, content of the check-in, and other competing time pressures. The leader ensures that the time limit for each person is set in advance and that someone is responsible for keeping track of time.

6. EVERYONE PARTICIPATES.

While people should have the option to pass if they do not want to speak, everyone should at least participate as an active listener. Eventually, people who have resisted the ritual will be less likely to pass and more likely to risk speaking. Leaders must participate, too. Leaders who exclude themselves send a message that the ritual isn't really important. They also miss out on its value.

The guidelines don't need to be repeated every time the ritual is performed; that reiteration would become tedious. The first few times, however, the leader may want to review the guidelines or ask someone in the group to review them. As with all rituals, the group may adjust the guidelines once they have tried the ritual for awhile. At the core, the whole point of guidelines is to create a safe and productive environment in which people can connect. Don't make the guidelines so complex that people fixate on following rules rather than relating to each other.

Depending on the time and goals of the group, the check-in process itself roughly follows a sequence designed to maximize participation. Because time is of the essence, each person generally goes through his or her whole check-in at once, then passes the turn to the next person. Of course, the group may choose to divide things up differently. Experiment a little. See what works best. The typical check-in will not try to do everything listed below, but will combine those elements that meet the organization's needs.

**POSSIBLE ELEMENTS
OF A CHECK-IN PROCESS**

1. Name
2. Feeling
3. Purpose
4. Task
5. Issue

---

1. NAME

This point may seem obvious, but names help keep people aware of each other's humanity, particularly when they are in a hurry or distracted. Names carry a lot of power and should not be undervalued. Starting their check-ins by stating their names should happen even in well-established groups.

2. FEELING

Offer two or three words that describe your feelings, for example: angry, glad, sad, afraid, scared, nervous, unsure, ashamed, or excited. Don't explain the feelings; just say what they are. Simply stating the feeling can help relieve the pressure to hide it or pretend that nothing's happening internally.

3. PURPOSE

Offer a sentence or two about why you're participating in this activity—not a task-oriented reason, but one that relates to your deeper purpose. "I'm here to discuss strategy" is less purposeful than "I'm here to help us develop the best possible strategy."

4. TASK

Offer a sentence or two to identify your objectives in the following activity or the day in general. Doing so helps other people understand your agenda. One person in a meeting might want to accomplish 20 goals in the meeting, while someone else may need to end or leave the meeting in ten minutes because she has a report to prepare. Declaring these issues at the beginning can help the leader manage time more effectively.

5. ISSUE

Sometimes it can be helpful to have people share concerns that are keeping them or the organization from performing well. As the list grows, group members may hear common concerns that they can now address collaboratively instead of alone. Some issues might be quickly addressed during the following meeting or activity while others may need time for discussion.

If the group is too large or time is short, the leader can break the entire group into smaller circles. Another time-saver is to do a check-in ritual in which people say their name and a one-word statement of feeling or a single phrase statement of purpose. If the ritual is performed regularly, these quick check-in rituals still connect people to each other and their task before they begin their activities.

Think back to the teacher mentioned above who was frustrated about an argument with her spouse. Imagine that when she arrived at school, she joined two or three other teachers for an informal check-in. They wouldn't even need a formal leader; their meeting would take just two or three minutes. As they went around the circle, she could tell them she was angry (statement of feeling) so that her emotions were not suppressed all day. Then she could say that she wanted to teach her students valuable lessons that can improve their lives (statement of purpose). Focusing on her purpose could help her concentrate more effectively as she headed off to class.

Some groups, such as construction crews, would most likely benefit from a check-in at the beginning of the workday. While some such crews might meet to receive orders from their crew chief or the contractor, a check-in would serve a different purpose. Rather than just receiving orders, crew members could connect with each other before heading off to the site. A large construction crew might find it helpful to break into work teams for a check-in. The roofers might pull together for a few minutes while the electricians did the same. You'll notice in the following example that the construction crew leader has added a statement about skill after determining that this would help people collaborate more effectively.

CONSTRUCTION CREW CHECK-IN EXAMPLE

1. NAME
Since construction workers are in a transient profession, saying names between jobs may help improve communication once on site. Since manual workers are often treated with disrespect by society, saying names could be one way for leaders to indicate respect for the crew.

2. SKILL
Each crew member could mention an area or two of expertise so that others could go to that person to ask a question or to seek good assistance.

3. TASK

Each crew member could indicate the part of the project for which he or she has responsibility or perhaps name today's primary goal. It might help everyone to know that the crane is arriving today or that the electrical system is being disabled.

Whatever the organization, the ritual of checking in can dramatically improve performance simply by helping people communicate more effectively about their needs, goals, and feelings. Though it may take a few minutes on the front end, checking in can save hours of misspent labor and misdirected communication. A sincere check-in energizes people and prepares them for success. It begins weaving the magical energy that comes with excellence, even before the activity has begun.

CHECK OUT

I THINK, WHAT HAS THIS DAY BROUGHT ME,
AND WHAT HAVE I GIVEN IT?

HENRY MOORE

After the work is done, people come back together to check out. This ritual provides a chance to reflect on the day or meeting that has transpired and to prepare for what comes next. The principle behind checking out is similar to that for checking in: it enables people to maintain an intense focus and energy around their contributions to the organization. By going through this process, people have a chance to acknowledge the incremental progress they have made toward the eventual success of their endeavors. They can also summarize lessons learned or concerns identified during the activity. In organizations committed to continuous improvement, check-out rituals provide a powerful means for compelling and marking that improvement.

Checking out happens at the end of the meeting or activity. Again, people gather and again their discussion goes around the circle, generally with the same people with whom they checked in earlier. The check-in guidelines apply to check-out rituals as well, except to add that check-outs can be harder to organize since people may want to hurry off to other activities or get home at the end of the day. Leaders need to be disciplined about the process and improve the efficiency of check-out rituals rather than skip them altogether. Leaving an activity with the energy provided by a check-out sends someone into their next task much better prepared. Leaving the work site for the day feeling energized and focused makes going home more pleasant and makes the prospect of returning tomorrow less daunting.

POSSIBLE ELEMENTS
OF A CHECK-OUT RITUAL

1. Name
2. Feeling
3. Accomplishment
4. Concern
5. Future Goal

---

1. NAME

Names are as valuable at the end as at the beginning of an activity or day. Saying them can help people reconnect after working together or separately.

2. FEELING

Feelings may have changed since the check-in. Sharing feelings at the end can help diffuse residual tension or distribute positive energy before leaving.

3. ACCOMPLISHMENT

People can share an accomplishment from the previous activity or a general sense of what has gone well. This step reinforces success and provides the opportunity for appreciation. Sometimes simply stating an accomplishment in front of colleagues is all of the public acknowledgment people need.

4. CONCERN

If people leave carrying a significant issue on their minds, the check-out enables them to let others know. Someone might feel that the meeting ended without addressing a key issue or that the activity was left incomplete. The concerns don't have to be addressed immediately, but at least the leader and others will know what they are.

5. FUTURE GOAL

Each person can share the most important "take-away" objective that comes out of the activity or meeting, ideally something that he or she looks forward to tackling. One person could state that she will work on her communication skills, while another might focus on getting some sleep to prepare for the next day's marathon session.

The ritual of checking out should energize people. It might conclude with a game or physical exercise to loosen people up and send them on their way feeling positive about what they have accomplished. At times, the check-out will reveal that the group is not performing well. Many people might leave feeling disappointed or frustrated. When that is the case—because it inevitably will be at some point—the leader shouldn't force people to pretend otherwise. Instead, the leader can ask them to contemplate the source of their disappointment and how each of them personally contributed to it. They don't have to discuss it immediately, but people can think about it as they leave. Rather than just dwelling on their negative feelings, reflecting on the causes of these emotions gives people constructive focus for their energy.

Organizational magic operates in subtle ways, and these one- or two-minute check-outs provide simple rituals through which leaders help people perform at their best.

CELEBRATE SUCCESS

EVERY BLADE OF GRASS HAS ITS ANGEL THAT STANDS
OVER IT AND WHISPERS, "GROW. GROW."

THE TALMUD

Anyone who has led people recognizes the value of celebrating success. Some organizations use annual meetings or employee-of-the-month awards to recognize contributions. Others broadcast deserving people's names through newsletters to inform and inspire their peers. Many organizations rely on financial rewards such as bonuses or profit-sharing plans to stimulate performance and reward its success. Ideally, every organization develops an incentive system that meets its strategic goals in relation to its industry, competitors, and business philosophy. The most magical organizations complement their systems with powerful rituals.

Rituals to celebrate success every day or at least every week can energize people and continually raise the bar of expectations. These rituals can keep both celebration and success in the forefront of people's minds. Celebration fosters positive energy and excitement, while success stimulates performance and innovation. When combined in rituals, they form a powerful team. The leader guides those rituals.

Rituals that celebrate success need to happen often, and several times each week is not too much. If time pressure makes once each week the only viable option, take that one time and make the most of it. Anything less frequent diminishes the power of the rituals to create an ethos of excellence.

The following story describes a ritual successfully used by one group to celebrate success regularly. Other more public and more sophisticated rituals marked important transitions and events during the life cycle of the organization. The one shared here was a simple ritual that could occur every day to maintain cohesion and promote high performance.

RITUAL KUDOS

Some people wanted to acknowledge others in the group who supported them each day, who generated great ideas, or who did something exceptional or did something ordinary exceptionally well. They proposed that each staff meeting should end with time for kudos. A kudo was a way of publicly thanking someone for doing something supportive or meaningful, something that helped the person fulfill a personal or organizational mission.

At the end of each meeting, people took turns speaking. They could either share kudos or pass. There was no official record keeping or designated number of kudos. The ritual worked because it was totally voluntary. In general, people listened intently to their colleagues and, at the end, the group applauded for each other.

Once the group started using the ritual, the energy of staff meetings changed considerably. Instead of focusing only on organizational problems or challenges, they made time to acknowledge the successes. People had been helping each other out anyway; kudo time was just a way to draw attention to that aspect of working together.

An unanticipated benefit was that so much positive attention was being directed toward the positive workers and contributors that little was left for the few loud negative people who might otherwise dominate the meeting. Over time, many previously passive members took a more active role in helping out their colleagues. Even the cynics who were initially skeptical of such a feel-good ritual eventually joined in both giving and receiving kudos.

There were no formal rewards for getting a kudo; the kudo was an end unto itself. The kudos helped supervisors get a better feel for the ways in which people were adding value to the organization's success. As kudos became a ritual within the meetings, people began giving them more and more on their own outside of the meetings.

The kudos ritual helped this group create a critical mass of positive energy. That critical mass makes all the difference. Too often, leaders don't take risks with rituals because they fear the wrath of a few cynics who think rituals are too strange. Courageous leaders go ahead anyway because they recognize that if the whole organizational culture is permeated by an ethos of celebrating success, their jobs as motivators and taskmasters become far easier and much more exciting. Most people will be swayed by the good energy to participate, and only a few diehards may hold on to their resistance.

GUIDE RITUALS

EXECUTIVE SUMMARY

I HAVE NO RECIPE FOR HOW TO COMBINE THINGS.
BUT YOU MUST BE SINCERE.
AND IF YOU ARE, STRANGELY, IT WILL SUCCEED.

ANDREE PUTMAN

The success of every organization depends on the effectiveness of the meetings and activities that govern its existence. Leaders use rituals to make every gathering special, not just for the value of having people feel good, but because rituals make organizations more potent by energizing and focusing people before, during, and after their meetings and activities. Those leaders who say that they don't have time to pay attention to ritual process are ignoring the tremendous impact that these processes can have on decision-making, planning, morale, and ultimately, personal performance.

Rituals that honor the organization's mission and vision remind people why they are about to meet, work, or play. A pledge exercise can solidify each person's investment in the organization's mission. Visioning links a powerful story to a common activity to emphasize the value of the latter. Purpose provides focus for people, helping them understand their roles—which may seem relatively small—in the big scheme of things. If everyone is prepared with this understanding, together they can propel the organization forward.

Check-in rituals also prepare people and organizations for success by helping people focus their energies before a meeting or activity. The check-in can look different, depending on the unique needs of the organization, though in general it should provide participants a chance to state their name and the issues that appear relevant to their performance in the matter at hand. Some groups might have check-ins for discrete activities, while others may hold one at the beginning of the workday. Following some common check-in guidelines helps the leader create a safe and productive environment in which people can connect.

Check-out rituals are similar, except that they provide good closure to a meeting or activity, which in a different way also focuses and energizes people for their next actions. Through the check-out, the leader learns about the different perceptions of the people involved in a project or meeting. This awareness provides an excellent opportunity to catch and address potential concerns before they spiral out of control. When people are eager to get to the next meeting or activity, leaders must be disciplined so that the valuable closure of a check-out can take place.

While every organization offers some sort of formal or informal incentive strategy, some leaders intensify their efforts to inspire people by incorporating rituals that regularly celebrate success. For example, one could end each staff meeting with a kudo session in which people can publicly acknowledge others for their assistance or performance. Since the leader does not lead it, such a process encourages peers to recognize each other voluntarily and without explicit attachment to more typical measures of performance. Whether following this model or another, leaders can create a critical mass of positive energy by celebrating what works. Those celebrations leave little time for nonconstructive cynicism.

For generations, athletes, military leaders, and religious leaders have relied on rituals to inspire, motivate, and focus performance. They can be powerful tools, and when evoked by a leader who is attentive to individual needs and awareness, can enhance personal performance at almost any level. The time invested in guiding rituals comes back to the leader multiplied, as meetings become more efficient and other activities become more productive. Better use of time, enhanced productivity, and stronger relationships: these are some signs of leadership magic.

FUNCTIONS
- Make every gathering special.
- Honor the mission and vision.
- Check in.
- Check out.
- Celebrate success.

BENEFITS
- Better use of time
- Enhanced productivity
- Stronger relationships
- More energized people
- More focused people
- Fewer distractions
- Greater clarity of purpose
- Critical mass of positive energy

GUIDE RITUALS

SELF-REFLECTION SURVEY

Circle where you are on the scale. Place a star where you would like to be.

		Never				Always
1.	I make every gathering special.	1	2	3	4	5
2.	I use rituals to improve effectiveness.	1	2	3	4	5
3.	I use rituals to honor the mission and vision.	1	2	3	4	5
4.	I use rituals to help people check in.	1	2	3	4	5
5.	I use rituals to help people check out.	1	2	3	4	5
6.	I use rituals to celebrate people's success.	1	2	3	4	5

OPEN QUESTIONS

Consider, discuss, or write about your thoughts and feelings.

1. Rituals that I have found effective are…

2. The most challenging parts of designing rituals are…

3. One new ritual I would like to try with my organization is…

4. My plan for implementing this ritual is…

 TAKE BOLD RISKS

Lead people and organizations boldly into action.

LEAD PEOPLE TO THEIR BEST
ASSESS THE VALUE OF RISK
TRUST YOUR INTUITION
BEGIN

LEAD PEOPLE TO THEIR BEST

ACTION IS NOT EASY IN THIS WORLD:
FORCES OF DOUBT AND INERTIA ARE EVERYWHERE,
EVEN WITHIN OUR OWN MIND AND BODY.
STILL, WE MUST ACT.

DAN MILLMAN

Life is short, precious, and worthy of the very best we have to offer. We cannot afford to waste our time drearily and habitually in merely settling for the safe and familiar. Life is a dynamic process, ever-changing, ever-moving. If we resist growing ourselves and our organizations into the most powerful and beautiful entities of which they are capable, we cheapen our lives by disregarding our opportunity to fulfill our deeper purposes with as much passion as they deserve and demand.

If our organizations' missions are truly grandiose and idealistic, and if our personal missions stretch us to grow and become ever more powerful, neither will be met by good intentions alone. At some point, leaders who consistently achieve what others thought unachievable dare their organizations to leap from their comfort zones into the unknown. They want more and know that, to get it, they must try the untried, venture into the unknown, and empower others to follow them courageously and skillfully.

Leaders who guide their organizations by studiously avoiding risk get exactly what they planned for—organizations that can sail only on calm seas, that do not know the thrill of accomplishing the outstanding, and that have chosen complacency in a world that is inherently dynamic. There is a place for such organizations amongst those who would choose job security over job meaningfulness or passivity over innovation. But eventually, even those people who want to cling to the status quo must face the reality of an ever-changing environment that destroys those organizations—and individuals—unwilling to acknowledge the vibrant dynamism of life. History and business textbooks are full of mournful stories about leaders and organizations that refused to consider the future. Plenty of people regret the leaps they never took; they sit on the metaphorical porch wondering, "What if...?"

Taking bold risks is highly personal. Each leader defines boldness and risk along a vast continuum. One leader's dramatic leap of faith might be another leader's daily drudgery. Much of the variance in these perceptions comes from each person's different experiences with safety and risk-taking. Some people have taken risks and been burned, and so they swear never to repeat that experience. Others might respond to the same event by wanting a second chance so that this time they can do it "right." For one leader, letting people work in teams might represent a huge risk because it means giving up some control. Another leader might be very comfortable guiding teams yet not be accustomed to giving direct commands. For that leader, the risk would lie in actually taking control in a more traditional manner. A high-tech company might risk becoming more people centered, while a people-centered organization might risk developing its technological infrastructure.

ASSESS THE VALUE OF RISK

COURAGE IS RARELY RECKLESS OR FOOLISH...
COURAGE USUALLY INVOLVES A HIGHLY REALISTIC ESTI-
MATE OF THE ODDS THAT MUST BE FACED.

MARGARET TRUMAN

Even the boldest leaders approach risk intelligently. There is no point in setting out foolhardily along a path without preparing to meet and overcome the potential obstacles. Bold risk-takers aren't stupid or excessively impulsive. To whatever extent possible, they create the conditions for their success before they leap. The seven practices that have been discussed thus far come before this one precisely because risk-taking is such an audacious activity, that to do it without proper preparation would be irresponsible. Those of us who have leapt before we were ready know the pain and stress that can occur if a leader lacks the tools necessary to leap effectively.

The most competent risk-takers do not like failure any more than the most risk-averse leaders. The primary difference is that the former are willing to take the chance of failure if it means that success will propel them forward. Risk-takers despise mediocrity. They hate to see an organization flounder in indecision and inaction just because of an outside chance that doing something innovative might not work out as planned. Mediocrity amongst people and organizations has no place in leadership magic except when it is a condition being analyzed so that it can be overcome. Leaders set the tone. If the leader tolerates performance that is familiar over performance that is effective, the organization cannot move toward its goals. There would be no where to go and no one to take it there.

There are some questions worth asking before a leader takes the organization into a bold new endeavor, or even before taking a more challenging risk with a single person. Though not a foolproof litmus test for risk-taking, these questions can help bring core issues to the forefront and enable the leaders and other people in the organization to make the best possible decision.

RISK ASSESSMENT QUESTIONS

MISSION

How does this potential risk reflect the organization's core mission?
How does this potential risk support my personal mission as a leader?

VALUE

What will be the value of this risk if it proves moderately successful?
What if it's extremely successful? Or only somewhat successful?
What makes this course of action the best one right now?
What negative consequences do we risk by taking this action?

IMPACT

Whom might this risk impact?

How do they feel about it? What do they think?

How much active support and resistance can I expect from others?

How do their perspectives affect my decision?

RESPONSIBILITY

What responsibilities might this risk require me to accept?

What responsibilities might this risk require other people to accept?

How much responsibility am I willing to accept for this risk? Why? Why not?

PASSION & COMMITMENT

Do I possess the passion necessary to go through with this task once I begin?

Am I committed to guiding this action through the potential rough spots?

Once leaders have assessed the value of the risk, they must make a decision. Sometimes, including other interested people in that process can be valuable; other times, leaders need to step away from the chorus of voices to gain clarity. Again, there is no single right way, though some organizations may find it helpful to develop a consistent decision-making and risk-taking process to guide leaders through those situations. A formal process can help ensure that good questions, including some of those listed above, are being asked by leaders who might be heavily pressured or biased by other competing concerns.

Still, no matter how many elaborate processes leaders have at their disposal, bold risks often come down to a "gut feel." They cannot always rely solely upon reams and reams of data, reports filed by numerous consultants and specialists, or flow charts, decision trees, and other helpful tools. Some organizations come to depend upon their data tools so much that they effectively take their leaders out of the decision-making process. In these organizations, leaders collect and enter data but let computer programs or outsiders make the final recommendations, and sometimes, by default, the actual decisions.

Dehumanizing or outsourcing the decision-making process makes a magical organization impossible to create. One can develop a very efficient organization, even a truly great one, but those leaders who remove themselves from the risk-taking process cannot inspire the best from their members because they no longer elicit the best from themselves. Once the leader has abdicated the very important and visible leadership function of taking risks, others will do the same. They will let their tools and processes make decisions for them, as if this somehow protects them from the risk of their own potential failure.

TRUST YOUR INTUITION

WHAT LIES BEFORE US AND WHAT LIES BEHIND US
ARE SMALL MATTERS COMPARED TO WHAT LIES WITHIN US.
AND WHEN WE BRING WHAT IS WITHIN
OUT INTO THE WORLD, MIRACLES HAPPEN.

RALPH WALDO EMERSON

Each of us is born with a powerful voice inside us. That voice guides us through our early years, allowing us to explore, develop relationships, and communicate. While young children, many of us are adventurers exploring the world, and adults look upon us with joy in their eyes as we struggle to crawl, form our first friendships, and take our first real steps on our own. We are the embodiment of that technical business term "continuous improvement" since every day is full of rapid physical, emotional, and cognitive growth. At that stage in life, learning and becoming our best is simply expected, and so it happens.

Then, for many of us, something begins to shift. We stop listening to that powerful internal voice and replace it with the external voices of family members, teachers, religious leaders, and the media. "Do this." "Stop it." "Don't touch." "No." "Wrong." "Bad." "You're crazy." "You're stupid." Though many of those speakers have our best interests at heart, few if any encourage us to develop a trusting relationship with ourselves, and some teach us to believe that we are worthless. If we are worthless, then we certainly shouldn't trust our inner voices. Indeed, the more insecure we become, the more we need to find affirmation outside ourselves.

The internal distrust that started in childhood gains strength through our formal education. Most schools are designed to ensure young people can follow orders, read directions, and perform fairly rote tasks. Few schools truly engage students to develop critical thinking skills that require they use their internal senses to analyze and interpret information. Even fewer cultivate the ability of students to tap their inner creativity. Most schools just aren't set up that way. Many people look back fondly on those precious few teachers who did encourage them to develop their unique qualities, to access the creative muse within themselves, and to hone their critical filters so that they could do something with all that information they were memorizing. Unfortunately, such teachers were often exceptions.

Along the road to leadership, many people learn to trust their intellects, technical training, or relationship skills. These competencies enable them to build and lead viable organizations that can pursue their missions well. Yet no matter how intelligent or well-trained a leader is, no matter how well he or she can work with others, these skills are not enough. Those leaders who consistently create leadership magic, whose organizations perform at their highest levels again and again, have also learned to trust their intuitions. Those leaders who have not earned their own trust find it much harder to earn the trust of others.

Rational analyses are helpful when cold hard data provides the answers that leaders need to make decisions. Yet many of the most complex situations that leaders face require the wisdom of their experience and knowledge. Intuition incorporates the experiences gathered over the years and organizes that information in a very complex manner. For some people, their intuitive side communicates very loudly and clearly, regularly guiding them through tough decisions. For others, the intuitive side remains very quiet either for lack of attention and practice or because of a greater reliance on concrete thinking. Those who depend more upon their intellects than their "guts" can still learn to use their intuition to gain the benefits of their intellect.

Each person's relationship with his or her inner voice is unique and faces distinct silencers that discourage it from speaking up or being heard.

These silencers can block each person's natural creativity, can keep people's energy from flowing freely so that they can give their best to their work, and can distract them from the most important issues before them.

The following antidotes to these silencers challenge the individual to strengthen his or her personal relationship with self. In performing these actions, leaders prepare themselves to better serve others. Though it may seem contradictory, dedicating time and energy to personal growth can be the most important step a leader takes in moving an organization to the next level of performance. The following strategies can help leaders develop the confidence in their voices that enables them to more effectively take bold risks.

TOOLS FOR DEVELOPING SELF-TRUST

➢ Make affirmations.
➢ Take alone-time.
➢ Write in a journal.

MAKE AFFIRMATIONS.

Some leaders develop statements that affirm their value by targeting an area in which they feel uncertain. Simply looking in the mirror at the beginning of each day and saying "I am trustworthy," can help someone believe in his or her own trustworthiness. The affirmation sets an internal expectation for the person, and many people rise to the expectations they set for themselves. Because the messages we tell ourselves are so important, leaders also need to eliminate the harsh negative messages they tell themselves such as "I am worthless" or "I am not dependable." While remaining honest about their challenges, leaders should avoid entering a downward spiral of destructive self-criticism. As they develop more confidence in their trustworthiness, they gain more trust in their intuition.

TAKE ALONE-TIME.

Many leaders dedicate hundreds of hours each month to meeting other people's needs. They listen, support, protect, serve, and give generously of their time and energy to help other people do their best. Amid all this action, many leaders do not make time by themselves. They cannot hear their own intuition because they are so immersed in other people's demands and needs. By taking time to be alone, leaders find the opportunity to silence many of those external voices and let the internal ones speak up. Some leaders take a few minutes each day by themselves, perhaps in meditation, or perhaps walking or exercising and letting their thoughts emerge. Others find it helpful to give themselves a personal retreat and take several days in the mountains, at the beach, or otherwise on their own. For some people, being alone is absolutely terrifying, which is why it becomes all the more important for them to practice being alone. Leaders who are not comfortable in solitude will face great difficulty, for at times their responsibility and commitment will cause them to be alone. At those points, they must trust their intuition to guide them and their organizations.

WRITE IN A JOURNAL.

Another way to develop trust in one's self is to take some time each week to write in a journal. The process of expressing one's self without fear of being graded or corrected for poor grammar in a space that is totally personal and confidential can help people develop stronger intuition. Sometimes putting thoughts down in writing helps clarify them and makes them more tangible. As people get to know themselves and their perceptions through writing, they find greater value in their inner voices and are more likely to trust themselves when they must depend on those voices.

A leader's most potentially powerful resource is his or her inner guidance. By nurturing themselves and understanding their own voices, leaders become more adept at anticipating and appealing to other people's internal voices. Learning to trust one's self requires many of the skills that build relationships with others. Leaders must care about themselves, be able to empathize with themselves, and develop a trusting relationship with themselves. As this development happens internally, it can then happen externally.

The inner voices of leaders not only provide the inspiration for taking bold risks, but also give the leaders the courage to be bold in the first place. People can't leap into the unknown with grace or skill when loud voices nag inside, declaring that they don't know what they're doing. Courageous innovators cannot envision new possibilities if they listen to every critic who insists that they are bound to fail. The sooner leaders strengthen their relationships with themselves, the sooner they become more effective leaders of their organizations.

BEGIN

WHATEVER YOU CAN DO
OR DREAM YOU CAN, BEGIN IT.
BOLDNESS HAS GENIUS,
POWER AND MAGIC IN IT.

JOHANN VON GOETHE

Before leaders take action, there is only potential. Visions, missions, ideas, concepts, and even material resources are of little value unless someone eventually translates them into relevance in the real world. Good intentions are fine, but what good is an intention that never manifests itself in reality? How has one made the organization any better by having a good idea that never finds expression, let alone realization?

To take action, leaders become change agents who transform the familiar into the new. They open a door through which the organization can experience new possibilities and practices. To be an agent of change is risky, for it places the leader in that intersection of possibilities where risk, potential, excitement, and fear come together in a surge of energy that frightens many people. Leaders who can hold that energy and move through their own fear enable their organizations to reap the rewards of innovation and adventure. They guide organizations that are continually energizing and energized by action.

Once leaders take action, they create positive momentum, which propels the organization confidently in the direction of its mission. As leaders continually demonstrate their willingness and ability to take bold risks, their confidence and strength can empower others to do the same. An organization made up of many people taking action, innovating, and looking for new ways to improve their effectiveness becomes ever more successful. Continuous improvement can happen precisely because so many people share it as a common goal. The resulting synergies appear magical to outsiders. Good things just keep happening. Some call it luck, yet the people who are taking bold risks recognize that luck comes from being prepared and courageous.

I remember the first time someone asked me, "So where do we begin?" The person wanted to know how to start creating magical organizations. In some respects, this entire book represents an answer to that question. Each practice contributes to the leadership magic of outstanding organizations, though ultimately, each leader is driven by different internal and external forces and, thus, must answer that question for him or herself.

In addressing how to begin, leaders consistently run into some common challenges, the two most rigorous of which are fear and isolation. Fear distracts people by focusing on the potential for failure. In some people, it creates a sort of vertigo, a sense that no matter how careful they are, they are bound to fail in anything they do. Leaders who plan and act in response to their fears allow themselves to be driven in a reactionary direction. There is no room for boldness when fear is in charge.

STRATEGIES FOR FACING FEAR

➢ Act despite fear.
➢ Begin with the easiest step.
➢ Begin with the hardest step.

ACT DESPITE FEAR.

Don't wait for fear to go away, because waiting doesn't usually help. Fear diminishes as people have more successful experiences, though if they keep pushing themselves to ever higher levels of performance, the fear might remain as a reminder of the unknown. Learning to move through the fear is essential. Anxiety does not need to be a block to action. When people make fear an incentive to act, they use the nervous energy to propel themselves forward. Fear can prepare people for success if they let it serve them.

BEGIN WITH THE EASIEST STEP.

Brainstorm a list of 10 possible actions that could begin a process. Choose the easiest. Do it. Choose the next easiest. Do it. By beginning with the easiest action and finding success, leaders can gain confidence in their ability to be successful. This strategy can create a cycle of growth and action within a person, as each positive experience prepares the person for the next one.

BEGIN WITH THE HARDEST STEP.

Brainstorm a list of 10 possible actions that could begin a process. Choose the most difficult. Do it. Choose the next hardest. Do it. By beginning with the most terrifying or daunting challenges, leaders sweep them out of the way so that they can free themselves of heavy or distracting anxiety. Successfully meeting the most difficult challenges can empower leaders to act more decisively and effectively in everything they do.

At the other extreme are those leaders who profess to have no fear at all. They, too, can be dangerous to their organizations because nothing checks their enthusiasm for an idea. Because they don't care about failure, they sometimes fail to take the necessary steps to prevent it. Leaders who never feel fear should surround themselves with people and systems that will compel them to assess their risks before they take them.

Fear increases isolation by keeping people from reaching out to others. Solitude can keep leaders from successfully taking bold risks because they deny themselves the practical and energetic support of other people. No matter how well leaders trust their intuition and no matter how skilled or intelligent they are, solitary leaders cannot take bold risks *for* their organizations. They can do so only *with* their organizations. Thus, breaking the habit of making decisions alone is essential.

STRATEGIES FOR FACING ALONENESS

➢ Find a mentor.
➢ Invite a partner.
➢ Let others join you.

FIND A MENTOR.

Ask someone for support, particularly if he or she has faced a similar situation before. Mentors do not do the work for leaders, but guide them through the process so that leaders benefit from the mentor's wisdom. Mentors can help leaders assess risks before they take them, and can encourage them to stay focused through the difficult times.

INVITE A PARTNER.

Ask someone to join in taking the risk itself. Partnerships spread the risk across two or more people so that one person does not bear the risk alone. Leaders can gain the benefit of the other person's energy, enthusiasm, and skill so that the boldness of the risk becomes less intimidating. Though partnerships have their challenges and limitations, they can help people accomplish tasks that they never would have faced on their own.

LET OTHERS JOIN YOU.

Take the first few steps, and then let others who have seen the power and potential of what you are accomplishing come join you. Some people need to see someone else take the risk before they are willing to join in or before they even realize that taking such a risk was possible. Leadership guides often speak about the value of creating an inspiring vision. For many people, the most compelling vision is communicated not in words but in action. When leaders take bold risks, they demonstrate their vision rather than just making promises. Action-oriented people will be attracted to action-oriented leaders.

At the other extreme stand those leaders who cannot take any actions alone. These leaders take action only when others around them validate them or even make decisions for them. They endanger their organizations by not believing in themselves and thus fostering a climate of distrust. Their lack of faith in themselves causes many people to wisely question their strength, particularly when difficulties arise. Leaders who are afraid to lead alone should plan strategically to develop the self-trust necessary to go forward.

Starting is the most important step of all. Leadership magic is not just a theory, but an action-oriented approach to bringing out the best in people and organizations. This book is built around practices because they require practice. Thinking about them is fine and perhaps necessary to build an understanding, but reading this book will prove valuable for leaders and their organizations only if the ideas herein are put into practice.

TAKE BOLD RISKS

EXECUTIVE SUMMARY

THE GREAT THINGS THAT HAVE BEEN ACCOMPLISHED
IN THIS COUNTRY HAVE BEEN BY PEOPLE
WHO HAVE COUPLED THE MIND WITH THE DEED.

GENE LANIER

Leaders have a tremendous opportunity because they can help create magnificent organizations that enable people to perform at their very best. With this opportunity comes audacious responsibility for the leaders have accepted the challenge and must prove worthy of the trust that so many others have given them. To settle for anything less would be negligent and an abuse of the power they have accepted. The world cannot afford to waste humanity's precious intelligence, creativity, and hard work; we need every possible contribution to make our world as healthy and vibrant as possible.

Leaders lead not only through words, but also through actions. Their actions demonstrate their commitments and intentions far better than promises can, because their actions model what they really believe. By assessing the value of risks before they take them, leaders minimize the likelihood of unnecessary mistakes. They make sure that the potential risk links to the organization's mission and adds value to it, consider its impact on others, clarify and choose responsibilities, and make sure they possess the passion and commitment necessary for success.

While organizations can create systems to assist in decision-making and other forms of risk-taking, ultimately, leadership depends on the individuals involved. Leaders must trust their intuition and know themselves well enough to ascertain their strengths and weaknesses. Leaders who are not worthy of their own trust have a difficult time earning the trust of others. By making affirmations, taking alone time, and journaling, leaders can develop greater confidence in their inner voices. The inner voices that guided us as children can help guide our organizations just as well if we practice them, and in some cases rediscover them after years of inattention.

Knowing how to take risks intelligently allows leaders to start out, and trusting their intuition makes them more powerful, but ultimately, they must simply begin. Leaders have to start taking action, or their good intentions will achieve nothing. Fear and isolation can pose powerful obstacles to beginning and must be faced rather than denied. As leaders begin taking action, they are likely to attract other action-oriented individuals, and, together, they create a wonderful synergy in the organization so that bold risks are taken at every level.

Out of bold risk-taking, leadership magic flourishes. Organizations that consistently move from success to success are those that avoid complacency by looking for the next strong possibility and pursuing it. When leaders dare people to approach the highest levels of creativity and innovation, they make their organizations lively collections of passion and ideas, and no matter what industry one serves, these assets make an organization more powerful and more viable over time.

FUNCTIONS
- Lead people to their best.
- Assess the value of risk.
- Trust your intuition.
- Begin.

BENEFITS
- Make more intelligent decisions
- Take more effective actions
- More opportunities for success
- Greater creative energy
- More action-oriented organization
- Attract more action-oriented people
- Generates more enthusiasm and commitment

TAKE BOLD RISKS

SELF-REFLECTION SURVEY

Circle where you are on the scale. Place a star where you would like to be.

	Never	Always
1. I take constructive risks.	1 2 3 4 5
2. I assess the value of risks before taking them.	1 2 3 4 5
3. I trust my intuition.	1 2 3 4 5
4. People describe me as "action-oriented."	1 2 3 4 5
5. People describe me as a "risk-taker."	1 2 3 4 5
6. Once I have a decent plan, I implement it.	1 2 3 4 5

OPEN QUESTIONS

Consider, discuss, or write about your thoughts and feelings.

1. Some of the best risks I have ever taken include…

2. Opportunities I have missed because I did not take the risk include…

3. One bold risk that I want to take is…

4. My plan for taking that risk is…

IMPLICATIONS

ACCEPT THE RESPONSIBILITY

THERE IS NOTHING MORE DIFFICULT TO PLAN,
MORE DOUBTFUL OF SUCCESS,
NOR MORE DANGEROUS TO MANAGE
THAN THE CREATION OF A NEW ORDER OF THINGS.

NICCOLO MACHIAVELLI

It may seem unusual to refer to quotes from both Machiavelli and Kahlil Gibran in a book that explores leadership magic. Yet that very juxtaposition between the cold hardness of the prince and the warm softness of the poet captures perfectly the complexity of what many leaders want to accomplish. They want their organizations to be excellent, yet recognize that excellence can only occur when people perform at their best. And people can consistently perform at their best only when organizations create the supportive conditions that enable them to do so. Thus, the individual and the group must look to each other to provide the support and value each of them needs.

Before rushing off to teach new terms and implement new practices, leaders should perform the same due diligence that they would apply to any major organizational decision. Before adopting new processes or teaching new leadership techniques, leaders need to assess whether or not they accept the responsibility of guiding their organization through different ways of doing things. For example, although conflict can serve a valuable purpose, I wouldn't envy the leader or the organization in which people are told to vent all of their conflicts without ever learning a process for doing so effectively. Nor would I want to follow the leader who likes the spirit of taking bold risks but skips the part about assessing the value of risk. Both organizations would endanger their missions and the people who are committed to serving them.

Before taking on new leadership responsibilities, leaders should go back to the chapter on taking bold risks and answer the questions designed to assess the value of risk. Accepting leadership duties is itself is a risk, and those questions can help leaders decide whether or not to move forward in introducing a leadership paradigm that may look very different from the one to which the organization has grown accustomed. Once the leader chooses to accept the responsibility for leadership magic, then the practices flow more easily.

START SOMEWHERE SIGNIFICANT

THE SECRET OF GETTING AHEAD IS GETTING STARTED. THE SECRET OF GETTING STARTED IS BREAKING YOUR COMPLEX OVERWHELMING TASKS INTO SMALL MANAGEABLE TASKS, AND THEN STARTING ON THE FIRST ONE.

MARK TWAIN

In this book alone, one can find many practical tools for leading effectively, and most leaders draw on many resources for their leadership strategies. So where do leaders start? How do they begin changing the culture of their organizations to make them even more effective, so that people perform closer to their potential? Leaders can't do everything and expect to do it well. The following guidelines to implementing these practices might be helpful, particularly as a warning for those leaders who are looking for a quick fix. Cultural change takes time.

GUIDELINES FOR LEADING CHANGE

1. Start by focusing on one practice, ideally one that can have a noticeable impact.

2. Choose a few people who want to improve the quality of the organization.

3. Work on that one practice with those few people.

4. Let other interested people join you voluntarily.

5. As people improve that one practice, move on to the next one. Let the next practice emerge from the needs of the organization.

6. Continue this cycle, focusing on achieving good results through voluntary participation.

7. Think about the long term. By considering the sustainability of the organization, leaders are more likely to ensure its short-term success at any given moment.

The world is hungry for leaders who can lead people to excellence. This is not a time to hold back but a time for action. Most of the action that organizations really need is not particularly flashy nor the stuff of dramatic newscasts. It is, rather, the kind of action that earns a leader credibility day after long day, as the sweet results of helping people become their best come trickling in at first, then rushing onward as the organization becomes one that is truly magical.

CONSIDER THE RIPPLE EFFECT

ALMOST ANYTHING YOU DO WILL SEEM INSIGNIFICANT,
BUT IT IS VERY IMPORTANT THAT YOU DO IT.

MAHATMA GANDHI

At a time when children commit horrendous violence against each other and when families struggle to stay together, it would be absurd to ignore the ripple effect of leadership magic. Rather than blaming the politicians or the media for our problems, instead of looking outside ourselves for a silver bullet or for some hero on a white horse to rescue us from our condition, we can each strengthen and heal the world simply by becoming the best leaders possible.

The leadership magic created within organizations can spill over into people's homes and communities. Imagine the family members who practices their listening skills or ability to empathize. Envision the schools that reduce alienation by teaching young people how to leverage diversity. Consider what might happen if neighborhoods created rituals to bring people together so that they knew and even trusted each other.

As people become better leaders within their organizations, they gain the power to take their leadership skills into their homes, neighborhoods, and schools. As their communities become better places to live, the organizations can become even more successful. The relationship between organization and community is no different from the relationship between people and organizations. The success of one is directly related to the success of the other. Leaders stand at that powerful junction where these entities meet, and through their honed skills, capable intelligence, and generous heart, they help create a world that is even a little bit closer to the best it can be.

A NOTE FOR ENTREPRENEURS

THE ENTREPRENEUR IS OUR CREATIVE PERSONALITY—ALWAYS
AT ITS BEST DEALING WITH THE UNKNOWN, PRODDING THE
FUTURE, CREATING PROBABILITIES OUT OF POSSIBILITIES,
ENGINEERING CHAOS INTO HARMONY.

MICHAEL GERBER

If you are beginning a new organization, people may advise you not to dedicate time thinking about the subtleties of leadership; they may say that your only concerns should be cash flow and getting your name out there. Beware of such advice, for it can cause you to miss out on high performance early on and cause headaches down the road when they say it's suddenly okay to start caring about the nuances of leadership. Implementing these leadership practices from the very beginning of an organization's existence can help it do everything else even more effectively. Obviously, cash flow and name recognition are valuable to most start-up organizations, and that is why it is *vital* that their leaders use leadership magic to make the most of their time, energy, and human resources.

I urge you to take advantage of your situation. At the beginning of forming an organization, its culture does not yet exist. There are no norms and few expectations because everything is just coming together. At that point, leaders can begin creating the culture so that it draws forth the very best in people. Once begun along those lines, the culture is more likely to perpetuate itself. When conflict is handled well from the beginning, less animosity gets buried or distracts people. When missions are aligned early on, greater synergy develops between the people who are establishing the organization.

Starting an organization is a daring and demanding task. It takes tremendous energy and commitment, and many times, people fail. Though nothing can make a start-up venture completely failproof, the practices of leadership magic support some of the most essential components of successful organizations. Entrepreneurs possess the courage to take bold risks; that same courage can help them lead others to excellence.

A LETTER TO READERS

Dear Readers,

I envision *Leadership Magic* serving as a catalyst for our growth—personal, organizational, and, ultimately, global. As you use these practices and integrate them into your life, you will emerge with important lessons about leadership. You will also continue to develop your overall skill base by trying new practices and refining old ones. Along the way, you will develop your own sense of what works and what doesn't. Your observations are invaluable, for they can provide essential guidance as we move forward.

As you practice the skills outlined in *Leadership Magic* and as you develop other skills, I encourage you to teach these abilities to others. We need as many mature, talented leaders as possible. Whether you write books and articles, mentor individuals, or lead group workshops, you can have a powerful impact. In everything that you do, you are a role model for leadership. That's how it works: we watch and learn from each other, which provides both opportunity and responsibility.

Please share what you learn with me as well. *Leadership Magic* is a small though significant piece of a very large puzzle, one that we must complete together if we ever hope to make the most of our human potential. As you come across strategies, stories, examples, or questions, please let me know. I am fascinated to learn what you have discovered. Some of these ideas may help provide impetus for future work.

Though writing is wonderful, my primary joy comes from working directly with people. My practical, experiential workshops provide an excellent opportunity to develop leadership skills in a safe, intense environment, one that is grounded in your organization's daily reality. My lively seminars and presentations engage participants by challenging them to think and practice leadership in the moment. I leave little chance for people to passively watch the clock.

I also enjoy investing in the success of organizations and leaders by establishing strong, mutually beneficial relationships. Meaningful change takes time—not necessarily lots of expensive hours, but certainly many intelligently used ones. If you're interested in learning more about working together through workshops, seminars, or long-term consultation, use the following contact information. By discussing both your needs and my competencies, we can be sure that we form a good match before collaborating.

You can reach me at:

Email:	magic@bvcmedia.com
Phone:	(303) 282-6493
Mail:	Ben Valore-Caplan
	c/o WordWorks Press
	1980 South Pearl Street
	Denver, CO 80210
Website:	www.bvcmedia.com

I am honored that you've chosen to read this book. Thank you.

Ben Valore-Caplan
Denver, Colorado
September 1999

RESOURCES

Bolman, Lee G., and Deal, Terrence E. *Reframing Organizations: Artistry, Choice, and Leadership*. San Francisco: Jossey-Bass Publishers, 1997.

Chopra, Deepak. *Creating Affluence. Wealth Consciousness in the Field of All Possibilities*. California: Amber-Allen Publishing and New World Library, 1993.

Cameron, Julia. *The Artist's Way: A Spiritual Path to Higher Creativity*. New York: Jeremy P. Tarcher/Putnam, 1992.

Cook, John, ed. *The Book of Positive Quotations*. Minneapolis: Fairview Press, 1993.

Covey, Stephen R. Covey. *The Seven Habits of Highly Effective People*. New York: Simon & Schuster, 1989.

Evans, James R., and Lindsay, William M. *The Management and Control of Quality*. Cincinnati, Ohio: South-Western College Publishing, 1999.

Fields, Rick, et. al. *Chop Wood, Carry Water: A Guide to Finding Spiritual Fulfillment in Everyday Life*. Los Angeles: Jeremy P. Tarcher, Inc. 1984.

Fisher, Roger; Ury, William; and Patton, Bruce. *Getting to Yes: Negotiating Agreement Without Giving In*. New York: Penguin Books, 1981.

Gardner, John W. *Excellence: Can We Be Equal and Excellent Too?* New York: Harper & Row Publishers, 1961.

Gerber, Michael E. *The E-Myth Revisited*. New York: HarperCollins, 1995.

Gibran, Kahlil. *The Prophet*. New York: Alfred A. Knopf, Publisher, 1923.

Heider, John. *The Tao of Leadership*. New York: Bantam Books, 1995.

Horn, Sam. *Tongue Fu! How to Deflect, Disarm, and Defuse Any Verbal Conflict.* New York: St. Martin's Press, 1996.

Kauth, Bill. *A Circle of Men: The Original Manual for Men's Support Groups.* New York: St. Martin's Press, 1992.

Kouzes, James M., and Posner, Barry Z. *The Leadership Challenge.* San Francisco: Jossey-Bass Publishers, 1995.

Millman, Dan. *No Ordinary Moments.* Tiburon, CA: HJ Kramer, Inc., 1992.

Moore, Robert, and Gillette, Douglas. *King, Warrior, Magician, Lover: Rediscovering the Archetypes of the Mature Masculine.* San Francisco, CA: HarperCollins, 1990.

——. *The Magician Within: Accessing the Shaman in the Male Psyche.* New York: Avon Books, 1994.

Moore, Thomas. *Care of the Soul: A Guide for Cultivating Depth and Sacredness in Everyday Life.* New York: HarperCollins, 1992.

Ondrejka, D. *Affective Pedagogy in Professional Education.* University of Denver: Unpublished Dissertation for Doctorate, 1998.

Peck, M. Scott. *The Different Drum: Community Making and Peace.* New York: Simon & Schuster, 1987.

Silko, Leslie Marmon. *Ceremony.* New York: Penguin Books, 1977.

INDEX